Happy Holidays
Christmas 2003
From
Mark & Margie Freeman

Tugboats 'n Towlines

THE MEN AND WOMEN WHO GIVE THEM LIFE

Warren Salinger

First published in the United States of America by:

Twin Lights Publishers, Inc.
10 Hale Street
Rockport, Massachusetts 01966
Telephone: (978) 546-7398
http://www.twinlightspub.com

ISBN 1-885435-42-8

10 9 8 7 6 5 4 3 2 1

Book design by
SYP Design & Production, Inc.
http://www.sypdesign.com

Printed in China

Ports of Call

Introduction

No history of the modern world—from the Industrial Revolution, to the invention of the steamship; the beginning of flight, to the Model "A" Ford—would be complete without the inclusion of the important role tugboats and their crews have played.

These pages feature tugs of varying sizes, and describe the many fascinating aspects of the tugboat industry. Delving in, you will quickly realize that tugboating may begin with the ship-assist work provided to inbound and outbound seagoing vessels—making possible most of our global trade in fuels, cars, machinery, bulk loads such as lumber, grains, cement, salt, mineral ores, etc.—but it certainly does not end there.

Tugs and their crews help build underwater tunnels and over-water bridges, piers and quays, and other waterfront structures, often helping to maintain them as well. Tugs and their crews push and tow barges of all sizes and configurations, filled with loads of products and materials, up and down the world's seacoasts and navigable rivers and even across vast oceans. They move barges filled with sludge wastes from major cities to prescribed ocean-dumping areas. And it is, most often, tugboats that are called upon to salvage the ocean's shipping wrecks before they sink.

Many a tugboat crew will tell you that their vessels are alive with colorful personalities experiencing all the moods of joy, anger, frustration and despair that most of us have felt at one time or another. Perhaps they are right. Yet none of them will deny that it is the women (not many) and men of the world's tugboat fleets who provide the skills, the commitment, the endurance—often under maritime conditions that are far from ideal—necessary to enable these boats to do the jobs that so much of our society unknowingly relies upon.

A fleet operator once told me that "without a skilled crew on those power platforms out there, you might as well have an outboard instead of a tug." Engineers make sure the engines hum. Deckhands move hawsers, lines and cables as though they had eyes of their own, slinging heaving lines to the decks of ships towering many stories over them, with an accuracy that defies description. Captains maneuver their vessels and their tows, factoring in currents, winds, tide changes, and competing traffic, as though they were parking their cars. Mates are a combination of all of the above. Almost everyone can do another person's job if required to do so, which occurs more often than you might think.

Tugboating is sometimes referred to as a job where hours of boredom are followed

Boston, Massachusetts

Portsmouth, New Hampshire

Portland, Maine

by shorter time frames so fraught with danger and adversity that only the coolest, most-experienced heads will prevail. Since damage to ships, tows, shore structures and to the tugs themselves is always extremely expensive and sometimes deadly, mistakes are avoided at all costs and seldom occur. Yet weather, every sailor's most-consistent threat, can part a tow at sea with little notice or make the docking or undocking of an ocean-going vessel a nightmare. Whatever the difficulty, tugboat crews always seem to rise to the challenge—overcoming dangerous situations only adds to their experience. Still, when tugboat crews ask for whom the bell tolls, they realize that one day it might toll for them.

This book is the culmination of visits to thirty United States seaports on all three coasts, and Lake Michigan, including eight of our top ports in terms of tonnage handled. Many of the tug crew members to whom I talked appear or are quoted in this book, but because of space limitations, many are not. Yet all have contributed significantly to my understanding of the American tugboat community.

This world and its global economy could not function without tugboats and their crews. *Tugboats 'n Towlines: The Men and Women Who Give Them Life* will tell you some of their stories.

Wilmingion, Delaware

Baltimore, Maryland

New York, New York

Hampton Roads, Virginia

Savannah, Georgia

San Francisco, California

HELEN MORAN

Seattle, Washington

Alaska

MAERSK ROCHESTER
LONDON

Boston, Massachusetts

San Diego, California

Portland, Oregon

Tacoma, Washington

Rockland, Maine

Boston, Massachusetts

Portland, Maine

Midway on the Gulf of Maine coast is Casco Bay—Portland's gateway to the sea. About forty vessels call here in an average month, half of them tankers calling at the Portland Pipeline Terminal, the other half a mixture of bulk, container and cruise traffic.

All of the crude oil discharged here finds its way to refineries in Montreal, Canada via pipeline. The reason for this circuitous routing is the severe weather which limits vessel traffic on the St. Lawrence Seaway during the winter months.

Because of its high volume of tanker traffic, many rules and regulations apply to the port of Portland—some driven by security, some by environmental concerns—and all have tightened over the years. Since the 1989 Exxon Valdez oil spill in Alaska, tugs here are now required to meet tanker traffic eight miles out to sea. Foreign-flag vessels with a draft of more than seven feet require a harbor pilot, as does domestic traffic from outside the Portland area whose skipper does not have "recency" for these waters (meaning that he or she has not transited them at least 12 times in the last 12 months as documented by the US Coast Guard). While docked, tankers need to have at least 16 lines running from ship to dock. They also require the boarding of a sea pilot while still seven miles out at sea. Security is much tighter in the world than it used to be.

In recent years, most of the ship-assist work in Portland has been done by Portland Tugboat and Ship Docking, recently acquired by McAllister Towing. A new company, Portland Tugboat LLC, has been formed with Captain Brian Fournier as president. Brian's dad, Captain Arthur Fournier, well-known in New England tugboat circles, continues as operations supervisor and is the senior docking pilot in the harbor.

Tugbitts, the quarterly journal of the Tugboat Enthusiasts Society of the Americas, recently wrote about Arthur Fournier: "His career started in the 1940s when he bought a sunken tug for one dollar, installed a GM 6-71 from a wrecked bus, and started a tugboat company in Boston Harbor around the *St. Theresa*, the first of many tugs. He has had close ties with McAllister, acquiring many of his early harbor tugs from them and working on various salvage jobs with them."

Tugboat events occur annually in many harbors, with fierce competitions in pushing and pulling contests as well as in tugboat races. This one, in Portland, Maine, pits the *Captain Sweet* against the *Eddie R.* on the waters of Casco Bay.

The Portland Pipeline Terminal handles an average of 20 tankers each month. The crude oil discharged here is headed for refineries in Montreal, Canada.

Portsmouth, New Hampshire

Captain Richard C. Holt, Jr.

Captain Richard C. Holt, Jr.

The seacoast community of Portsmouth, New Hampshire was first settled in 1623. Some say that its 23,000 people can lay claim to living in the third-oldest city in the United States. The Portsmouth Naval Shipyard, built in 1800 as the country's first such facility, is actually located across the Piscataqua River in Kittery, Maine. It has served as one of America's premier submarine building and maintenance facilities for more than 50 years. The Piscataqua River separates the states of New Hampshire and Maine and some believe that crossing the several bridges that span it, heading north, will not only bring you to a new state, but to a new "state of mind".

Though, at times, its appearance can be friendly and inviting, the Piscataqua River rips through its channel with both incoming and outgoing tides having currents measuring between two and a half and five knots, making it one of the three most swiftly running navigable bodies of water on the east coast, right behind Massachusetts' own Cape Cod Canal and Hell's Gate on the East River in New York.

Portsmouth is home to Captain Richard C. Holt, Jr., a handsome, strapping young man in his late thirties. Since he is one of the port's three active harbor pilots, the Piscataqua River is his working home as well. Dick is a native son, a product of Portsmouth's schools and a 1986 graduate of Maine Maritime Academy. His father, Dick, Sr., preceded him at Maine Maritime in the class of 1958 and spent several years in the US Navy. Tugboating and piloting have been in the Holt family for many years. In his own youth, Dick Sr.'s father, a pilot and a tugboat captain, was urged to join the Navy in 1942, soon after the attack on Pearl Harbor. He was assigned to the Portsmouth Naval Shipyard as a warrant officer to teach Navy bosun's mates how to drive a tug, and was then sent to Pearl Harbor to work on salvage operations until 1945. Soon after the war, in 1946, Dick, Jr.'s grandfather, together with a local businessman, started Portsmouth Navigation. Prior to that time, most commercial shipping destined for the port of Portsmouth was assisted up river by Navy tugs. But as the ships grew larger and power plants and other commercial sites were developed on the waterfront, more tugs of larger proportions were needed. Richard Holt, Sr. joined his father's company in 1961. Three years later his dad, S. H. Holt, Jr., died. In 1967 Moran Towing, one of the country's largest tugboat firms, acquired the operation, and the Moran tugs stationed in Portsmouth harbor today have become a local landmark. The roots of today's Portsmouth Pilots, Inc. run deep and true.

"My grandfather died of cancer at the early age of fifty-three, which resulted in my dad getting an early discharge from the Navy so that he could come back to Portsmouth to train as a harbor pilot. This was in the early 1960s. Another pilot named W. H. Barker was killed in an auto accident on the Maine Turnpike. There are three of us today—my dad, myself and our colleague, Matt Cote, who has been on board for about 22 years.

"I grew up with the tugs. Years ago, my dad was the manager here, and as soon as I was old enough to work, I came aboard the boats to do what deckhands spend so much of their time doing: chipping and peeling paint. I remember a tug called the Captain Bill *up in Portland, Maine—formerly the* Marie Moran—*and recall cementing her ballast and water tanks. During my early years and even while at Maine Maritime, I always wanted to learn as much as possible about the deck jobs. At the Academy, that was called 'nautical science'. There was some curiosity about the engine room, of course—but I always wanted to drive the tugs more than I wanted to run them!"*

Following graduation from Maine Maritime, Dick had a brief career as a deck officer on a tanker, the *ARCO Fairbanks*, but he soon realized that he could reach his goal of obtaining a master's license more quickly by returning to the tugboat community with which he was already familiar. By age 23 he had accomplished his mission of adding a 1600-ton master's license to the third mate's rating he already held by virtue of his Maine Maritime degree. That tonnage is more than adequate for almost all tugs because of their relatively low displacement.

We talked aboard the Moran tug *Fells Point* which has a displacement of 264 gross tons. A single-screw vessel with a 2400HP ALCO engine, she was built in 1956 at the Equitable Shipyard in Madisonville, Louisiana. After lots of Navy work in Norfolk, Virginia as well as regular harbor duty there, she found her way to the Piscataqua. As one of the four Moran tugs in Portsmouth today, she assists the nuclear powered *Los Angeles*-class attack submarines, which still move in and out of the Portsmouth Naval Shipyard for overhaul and refueling. She also works the occasional Navy barge needing help when the yard's own smaller tugs are not powerful enough, but mostly moves commercial shipping up and down the river as needed.

Harbor pilots often come out of the tugboat experience and Dick Holt, Jr. is no exception. When asked about the pilotage of inbound ship traffic, Captain Holt responded:

"If the vessel is a repeat visitor to the area, which about 60% of the traffic seems to be—the Irving tankers, the Melvin Baker III, the CSL Atlas, the liquid propane gas (LPG) ships like the Helice, the Havis, the Havfrost, the Helios, all of which head for our storage facility called the C-3 Terminal—we meet these ships about one mile east southeast of the 2KR buoy which marks the entrance to the river. If the ship hasn't been here before, we generally go out about a mile further.

"Many of the ships will be anchored awaiting the proper tide timing. Our tides tend to run about nine feet on the ocean-side of the channel and about seven feet up-river, both tide range and current speed depending on the phase of the moon. With the Piscataqua running as swiftly as it does, we try hard to reach the dock during 'slack tide' when the tides change. Normally that is about a ten-minute period, with perhaps another ten minutes

Zachery Reinauer has found her way to Portsmouth's Piscataqua River to pick up a tow headed for New York City. The Piscataqua River is one of the three swiftest navigable bodies of water on the east coast, along with Hell's Gate waters in New York and the Cape Cod Canal in Massachusetts.

on either side of mean slack tide when the current may only be running at about one knot. So our goal of timing to reach the dock is that 20- to 30-minute window. And, because this is such a rapid tidal river, meaning that at or near full moon, the water speed may be five knots, the docking procedures need to consider the fact that every six hours the direction of the current will change. That's what makes the Piscataqua so different from the Mississippi, for example, which may also run very quickly, but always in one direction!

"In addition to a bunch of docks at the shipyard, we have eight berths to reach up the river, starting with Granite State Minerals. In upstream order they follow as: the New Hampshire State Pier, the National Gypsum dock, shared by Irving Oil, Public Service of New Hampshire's two docks, the Simplex or Tycom Terminal for fiber optic submarine cable, Sprague Avery Lane which houses Pike Asphalt, Sprague Gasoline and the C-3 Propane Terminal, and Sprague River Road, the busiest dock, which receives cement, caustic soda, bulk fertilizer, salt, almost any kind of bulk material, as well as tallow (also called 'yellow grease'—any animal fat as a liquid), heating oil, kerosene, diesel oil and jet fuel. You can imagine that, the further upstream the ship needs to travel, the harder it is to meet that goal of reaching the dock at slack tide. The port of Portsmouth handles about 250 ships and barges a year or between 20 to 25 in an average month.

"We have Great Bay further upstream into which seven rivers flow. So even though the water at the lighthouse may be up high to its nine feet, it may only be five feet further up because it can't run through the river fast enough to equalize simply because the river is not wide enough or deep enough to handle the flow of that water. When the water at the lighthouse starts to go down as the tide goes out, it may still be lower up river. It generally takes two hours to equalize. Average draft at our eight docks is 36 feet, with the C-3 Terminal at 37.

"We also closely follow the 'three-two-one' rule recommended by the Coast Guard and the docking terminals. That means we have to have three feet of water beneath the ship's keel at the bar when we board it, two feet for the transit through the river, away from ocean swells, meaning that the ship is not going to rock, roll, pitch or yawl and one foot at the berth at low water. At high tide, that means we have an extra nine feet of water under keel out there and seven extra feet in the river. The shipping channel is 35 feet deep at low water. So at low water, we can only bring in ships with 32-foot draft requirements, because you need the three feet under keel.

The bulk carrier, *Agia Sofia*, at Portsmouth's Granite State Minerals pier. Often these bulkers deliver salt or salt mixtures to this facility, used to keep New Hampshire's roads as clear as possible during the long and often severe winter months.

"We usually get 24-hours notice of a vessel's arrival through the ship's agent. In our area, that is often Moran Shipping out of either Boston or Portland, which, by the way, is no relation to Moran Towing. These vessels don't just show up out of the blue— someone has ordered and is expecting their cargo. As soon as we get notified of their ETA (estimated time of arrival) and learn of their draft requirements, we plan their journey upstream according to the tides and dock availability, and notify their agent who in turn then makes the necessary arrangements at the receiving end. That means arranging for line handlers, customs, immigration, all the legal services, etc. Ships need to have clearance before they can enter any United States port, which means their

histories, safety records, etc., have to be checked out by the Coast Guard. Often, especially in winter, tankers may be coming up from Venezuela to Canada and get last-minute orders to turn west and head for Portsmouth. Well, they can't just expect to steam in. Berthing may be unavailable for several days if the dock space is already occupied and clearance checks first have to be performed. The ships may be anchored for several days, not always a pleasant spot to be on the North Atlantic's winter seas! As the vessel gets closer to us and we begin to have more-direct conversations with her skipper, we can often tell how familiar they are with our waters by their level of comfortability during those exchanges or how anxious they seem to be to find their tugs and pilot. The less sure they seem to be, the further out we will meet them. The procedures for departing outbound shipping are pretty much the same, only in reverse."

The shipping channel on the Piscataqua River is fairly wide, with its narrowest point, from the I-95 bridge to the Public Service Power Plant, measuring 400 feet.

"That sounds like a lot of width but it isn't when you consider the turns the channel takes and the moves to port or starboard that the big ships have to make in order to get to the docks farthest upstream.

"Then, when they leave, they have to be turned around, which is an even bigger problem. Trying to turn a 750-foot vessel in an 800-foot turning basin is pretty restrictive and needs to be done very carefully and safely. After all, we are protecting the port, the ship and its owner and the environment. For the bigger ships, more than 45,000 tons, we normally do this in the daylight but smaller vessels can usually come or go night or day. Of course, weather conditions, especially winds and tides, are always a concern.

"Here in Portsmouth, the tugs are also the pilot boats. We use the ship's power up or down river, often moving at speeds of four to six knots, with the tugs acting more as 'bending' tugs, helping to turn the ship, than as tow boats. Our jobs here also last longer than most of the work in Boston or Portland. First of all, it's a thirty-minute ride out to the vessel, then usually one and a half hours or so upriver and then another hour for docking while the freighters or tankers get their docking lines set. Most of the ships use about 18 dock lines, taking into account the swiftness of the river and the fact that the current runs

Moran Towing Corporation has tugs stationed in Portsmouth to handle much of the 40-50 monthly inbound and outbound vessel traffic. *Eugenia Moran, Fells Point, Carly A. Turecamo* and *E. F. Moran* have become the unofficial logo of the city.

out and then in continuously. Two tugs are most often assigned to vessels under 40,000 tons, three for larger ships. The propane ships require four tugs."

We talked on a beautiful late-summer day as the calmly flowing river mirrored the sparkling blue sky above it. But it didn't take too vivid an imagination to recognize the difficulty of boarding inbound traffic on seas churned by winter storms.

"We're lucky because these tugboats have submarine fenders which are designed to meet the convex hulls of Navy submarines under water. So when you come alongside a ship that is rolling while the tug is also rolling, occasionally they will hit below the water line which will cushion the impact. If it is too rough out there, we will get the ship under-way and advise it to turn to make a lee, creating some protection from the worst winds and seas. Then we will board on the leeward side. It's not comfortable in 15-foot seas and you can get awfully wet, but these tugs can handle almost any sea condition. Safety is always a major concern as the pilot clambers up the Jacob's ladder. The two biggest dangers are getting crushed between the tug and the ship's hull or having the fenders of the tug tear at the rope ladder while you are climbing it, snapping it and sending you and the ladder into the sea. Of course, there are sometimes wind and/or sea conditions during which we will simply not conduct a boarding and, perhaps because safety is such a big issue amongst us, we have never had a problem.

"Generally speaking, because the vessels are usually heavier with cargo while they are inbound, bringing them in is harder than taking them out. But if a ship is only half loaded with 15,000 tons of cargo and leaves several days later with 14,000 tons of ballast, there is not a big difference. Again, getting them through the bridges is the hardest part of the job. The first bridge heading up to Great Bay, the Memorial Bridge, is pretty easy because it has a 250-foot span and faces true to the currents, meaning that the water flows per-pendicular to the bridge opening. The next one up, even though it has a 200-foot span, is built askew to the current so that the opening beneath it as it pertains to a ship's passage shrinks down to 150 feet. It's a challenge to get a 750-foot vessel through there—but I've been doing this as a pilot for ten years now and you do get used to and comfortable with it. However, it takes a lot of time and training. You can't hurry experience!"

Dick Holt, Jr. has spent time on other waters as well. In the fall of 1986, he worked for Moran of Texas on the *Doris Moran*, a tug with nine crew members, which included a captain,

The bulk freighter *Xanadu*, with a Malta registry, at the Granite State Minerals dock. There are seven other berths up river from here, plus several more at the Portsmouth Naval Shipyard. The shipyard is actually across the river in Kittery, Maine, and, though downsized from its peak activity in earlier years, still does a great deal of maintenance and overhaul work for the US Navy's nuclear submarines.

first mate, second mate, two AB's (able bodied seaman), an ordinary seaman, two engineers and a cook. That large a crew was needed because they were towing a 30,000-ton, 150,000-barrel oil barge, the *New York*, through the Gulf of Mexico. He did this for two and a half years.

"Towing that large a barge between Texas and Florida ports was interesting. And, occasionally, Moran would put a different tug on that barge and we would sail up to Virginia to tow 'dead ships' from the Jamestown mothball fleet to the shipyards. I've also worked in the Caribbean, towing grain barges to countries like the Dominican Republic and to San Juan, Puerto Rico. For three years I did harbor work on the Miriam Moran in New York harbor. And I've had my share of heavy weather as anyone does who works at sea: northeasters off of Cape Hatteras...heavy seas in a northwest gale off of Norfolk, Virginia, causing a barge we were pulling down the east coast towards Mobile, Alabama to part its three-inch towing chain due to excessive chafing. Those are the experiences that teach mariners to think quickly and improvise solutions to problems that, if not fixed, can lead to pretty serious situations. When you have a heavy tow 800 feet behind the tug and other ocean traffic heads your way on a collision course and you can't raise the other vessel on the radio—which, by the way, though it isn't supposed to happen, occurs more frequently than you'd think—you better know how to take the proper evasive action quickly and effectively. And if that happens as you are moving through an oil field in the Gulf, as it sometimes does, you better know how to execute those maneuvers instinctively. Those are the close calls that make you pay attention and provide you with the experience you need in tugboating or piloting."

Having crossed the Piscataqua River many times during the years I have lived in New England, I have often glanced to the east and west to see what type of ocean shipping I could spot on its waters. Dick Holt, Jr. has given me a better understanding of how those ships arrive at their destinations—and a higher level of admiration and respect for the tugboat crews and river pilots who guide them there.

Carly A. Turecamo shoves off for a barge job across the Piscataqua River. She is a single-screw 2400HP tug, very much at home on the busy river that separates the states of New Hampshire and Maine.

Pat Kelly

Captain Pat Kelly

Her dad was a USAF fighter pilot, so she was no stranger to the military way of life. By 1976, Pat Kelley had enlisted in the United States Coast Guard, which led her into a four-year hitch with duty assignments on the Merrimack River, Newburyport and Boston, all in Massachusetts. No accident then that she decided to enter the Massachusetts Maritime Academy. Pat went to sea for five years, first as an AB, then as a third mate, working mostly on container and RoRo (Roll on-Roll off) vessels.

"It seemed like almost every ship I ever sailed on had a fire. While still at Mass Maritime, the Academy ship had an engine-room fire during which a cadet was killed. I had just come off watch and heard the news on the way home. The second fire was at sea on the Maine Maritime Academy ship which Mass Maritime had borrowed because of the first fire. This one was caused by a cadet smoking in the number five hold, which was filled with mattresses, all of which burned. We fought that blaze for an entire Sunday and ended up throwing smoldering mattresses overboard all over the Gulf of Mexico. The last fire was on a SeaLand ship that had a stack fire while docked in New York harbor. I had just come back from a couple of hours ashore to see fire engines everywhere!"

Perhaps it was the fires, perhaps her deep-sea sailing experience had been satisfied, but by 1988, Pat decided to set down more-permanent roots in Boston, bought her first tug and founded "Kelley Marine Transportation." Her first boat, the *Sea Horse,* was 50 feet in length, twin-screws, built in Houma, Louisiana, and was immediately put to work on Boston's Central Artery Project, helping in the construction of the Ted Williams Tunnel.

"The best part of that job was moving the tunnel sections out to their drop point. They would come in frames from where they had been built—somewhere down in Baltimore, I believe. They would be filled with cement until there was six inches of freeboard. It would take six tugs to get one section into the lay barge even when all six boats were really putting the coals to it! The construction manager acted like a docking pilot, giving commands to the tugs. He was great at that kind of communication, really good on the radio. At the proper time, the sections would be lowered into a trench that had been dug at the bottom of the harbor and divers would be sent down to connect them. Eventually, air would be blown into the newly lowered sections and the finishing crews would begin their work, completing all the needed infrastructure. Now completed, the tunnel has 42 feet of water between its top and low water."

Two 36' crew boats, *Seaview* and *Island Run,* soon joined the fleet and operated under a joint-venture charter agreement with Boston Transportation and Towing. They were assigned to work on the construction of the Deer Island Sewerage Treatment Plant, running personnel and equipment on several daily trips between the Fore River staging area in Quincy and Deer Island. In addition to ferrying the workers, they would pull barges that carried heavy equipment needed on the project. Like many tugboat jobs, it often got boring.

"We would pray for fog so that we could practice our navigation. Occasionally, the weather would get rather heavy and we worked through all of it including the famous October 'No Name' storm that became known as 'The Perfect Storm.' Those kinds of situations helped break up the boredom!"

After selling her company in 1996, Pat took time off to adopt two daughters and has recently become the manager of the Wentworth by the Sea Marina in Portsmouth.

"It's a great job. My daughters, Jesse and Samantha, four and two, now ride the launches with me and I get home every night. Not bad for an old USAF brat. But I do miss the tugs—they get into your blood. When the urge gets too strong, I try to arrange a ride-along on one of the Moran tugs docked in Portsmouth that handle most of the ship-assist work on the Piscataqua River. Once a mariner, always a mariner!"

Tug Alley Too, (opposite) recently converted from a working tug, now sails for Bob and Natalie Hassold's unique tug-related business, "Tugboat Alley." She may be chartered for sightseeing trips up and down the Piscataqua River, for weddings and/or other family events. Call 603-430-9556 or via the web at www.tugboatalley.com.

24

Boston, Massachusetts

Captain Conti Coluntino

Captain Conti Coluntino

While docking the tanker *Ioannis*, aboard the tug *Alex C*, (now the *Draco*), Captain Conti Coluntino, co-owner of Constellation Towing and Marine, Inc., presses hard against the tanker's port beam. He explains the rules that require double hulling on tankers to prevent serious oil spills:

"See where this vessel's cargo is stowed?," he says, pointing to areas clearly marked on the hull. *"Cargo areas require the double hulling—but where the ship's own fuel supply is stored is exempt from that requirement. So a tanker travels with cargo for only 50% of the time, right? So why the discrepancy?"*

Good question.

Russell Tripp, Coluntino's former boss and a Boston waterfront legend:

"Regulations too often are made by politicians who really don't know much about the problems crews face. A new one recently passed by the Coast Guard is that you have to have certified towing gear. What do they know about what certified towing gear really is? I had an argument with a Coast Guard officer about the strength of my hawser. I told him, it really doesn't matter. He said, 'Russell, don't you think you should know the strength of your hawser?' I said—'it doesn't matter.' He said 'well, why doesn't it matter?' I said, 'let me give you a scenario. I'm heading into the Cape Cod Canal with a 300-foot barge behind me. I'm on a 3,000HP tug in a five foot sea with 150 feet of hawser out and there is a five-foot heave. How much strain am I putting on it?' He said 'I don't know.' I said—'well, neither do I—what difference would a certification of towing gear make?'

"It always gets back to common sense. If I am pulling a barge with a ten-inch line and I don't have enough line out, there is going to be too much strain and I am going to pull out the bitts on either the tug or the barge. Only experience will tell you how much line is enough. Only experience!"

The crew on board the inbound tanker *Maersk Rochester*, fully loaded with refined fuel and very low in the water, receive a heaving line from the tug *Little Joe*. Feeding through the chock, the heaving line is attached to a ship's line which will be wrapped around the bitts on the tanker. Once that is done, the deck-hand on the tug will secure his end of the line to the tug's bitts, assuring a snug fit between the two vessels as they proceed towards the dock.

The McDevitt Girls

Women captains in the American tugboat community are rare. You might find one or two in various ports around the country, but in Boston there are three in one family! Fondly known as the "McDevitt Girls," one of their brothers, Mike, has his own tugboat which carries this name.

The McDevitt's grew up on Peddock's Island, located off of Hull, Massachusetts, a Boston suburb. Their dad moved the family, including baby Ed, to the island when he became the caretaker there. He soon added the job of Hull harbormaster to his portfolio and an additonal three kids—Michael, Christine and Judy—to his family. There was no electricity or running water but as the younsters grew, they developed a penchant for the sea, learning how to row soon after they had perfected walking. Before long, they were driving motorboats, then harbor launches, and soon Boston harbor commuter and sightseeing vessels had McDevitts at their helms. Today all four children and mom are tugboat captains.

Captain Judy McDevitt, senior got her start when a dredging company began working off of Peddock's Island in the early 1970's. Having learned a lot about seamanship from living offshore, it was no problem for mom to begin piloting one of the tugs in the dredging fleet. In those days, a license for that kind of work was not required but, in1975, the US Coast Guard changed the rules.

Captain Judy McDevitt, Sr.

> *"All four kids followed my lead,"* says mom, *"almost like getting their degrees from high school. I spent most of the 1980's doing dredging and construction work on the Chesapeake Bay.*
>
> *"It was my son Edward who really managed to get the rest of us into our tugboat careers",* says Judy, her squint frozen into her face, framing the steel blue eyes that have seen so many years on the water. *"He started with wooden tugs but I helped him buy his first steel boat, the* Fort Andrew, *back in 1984. Today both he and Michael own their own tugs."*

When we met, both mom Judy and daughter Christine were working as captains for Boston's Bay State Towing Company, whose owner, Russell Tripp, was a fixture on Boston's waterfront. Tripp accepted work that other companies often refused and so anyone who worked for him became experienced not only at ship-assist work but also in towing, salvage and rescue work. Asked about a particularly memorable job, mom Judy responded:

Captain Judy McDevitt

> *"It was three days before Christmas in the late 1980's when we got a call from the Coast Guard about a tanker that had broken down in Halifax, Nova Scotia. Because of her condition, the Coast Guard would not let the vessel depart under its own power, which meant that she had to be towed. They were not successful in getting anyone on the east coast to do the work, so Bay State Towing accepted the challenge. It was rough rounding up a crew to sail on such short notice, three days before Christmas but, along with Russell, Bob Clement and Alan Robson, I eventually signed on to leave for Halifax.*
>
> *"It was an epic voyage. We left Boston in a gale and arrived in Halifax three days later with winds running steady at 70 knots, gusting to 100. Seas were running 40 to 50 feet, which was higher than the* Russell Junior's *39-foot mast! We went to sandwiches for food—those of us who were still eating—and tried to sleep on a mattress on deck because you could not stay in your bunk—those of us who were still sleeping. The worst was that the toilet came back up at you like a damned bidet!*
>
> *"Departing Halifax on Christmas morning, we took the ship down towards Cape May, New Jersey, with Panama as our eventual destination. We were towing her on a 1500-foot long 9" nylon hawser that had to be spliced to reach that length. With December's frigid temperatures in the North Atlantic, that hawser froze stiff as a board and we had to get it into a heated area on the tug to thaw so that it could even be spliced. It took about two*

Captain Chris McDevitt

hours of beating to get it sufficiently warm. Then we joined the thimbles on the ends of the nylon line with a 100-ton towing shackle.

"When the seas were such that we could actually look and see the shackle out of the water, we knew it was time to slow down. Our speed when the ship's engines were running was about eight knots and when the tug's power was all we had, we were probably doing five. The day before we came to Cape May, with a strong wind blowing from the northwest, we sought out the lee of the shore. During the voyage down the coast, Russell actually told them how to repair their engines. We wanted to come alongside to give them some needed parts but never could because of the seas and ended up passing them across from ship to ship with a line and bucket. By the time we got close to Cape May, they had it done, so we let them go and off they went!

"According to Russell, the problem had been that the ship was riding so shallow that they were taking air into their sea suctions and they couldn't bleed it off. So he had them install bleeders that went out into the engine room and they eventually sucked out the unwanted air.

"That was a memorable voyage. We have participated in a few rescues of ships that have become disabled at sea. Went to a fire once, off the coast of Gloucester, involving a tug that was towing a ferry boat. Rescued a barge that had gone aground off Brewster. But, by and large, our towing work makes memories only when rough weather interferes and our work inside the harbor here, always aware of tides, winds, currents, is fairly routine."

Captain Chrissy McDevitt remembers a classic salvage job of a fishing boat off of Race Point on Cape Cod, Massachusetts.

"Oh yes, separating fish from fans and other equipment in the middle of winter was not a lot of fun. The seas were so high they went right over the pilot house. But it was memorable!"

She is her mother's daughter—a professional skipper, committed to the sea—and she has just earned her undergraduate college degree. Mom is taking courses too, with the goal of becoming a writer.

Captain Judy McDevitt, junior, youngest of the McDevitt children, maneuvers her small tug *Anna* up and down the Taunton River in Fall River, Massachusetts. *Anna*, is three years old and was built in Panama City, Florida. She is owned by Modern Continental Construction Company and is assigned to the building of a new highway bridge over the Taunton River. "Judy Two," as she is known, has spent quite a bit of her tug time doing construction work, including four years in Boston's Fore Point Channel working on the city's Big Dig project. She is every bit as gentle and as good in pushing construction barges around—whether they are loaded with derricks or with steel for the bridge or whatever—as her older sister and mother are when they are handling the big ships.

"I drove a launch boat around in Hull when I was 12 years old and got my first captain's license when I was just 18. Actually, the Coast Guard had made a mistake in giving it to me because 19 is the correct age—so I had to wait a year befoe I was legal! Commuter boats to Boston were my next jobs and in 1991 when I was 23 I started working the construction jobs, which I really like. Chrissy and mom are almost always on call and never know when they will be working. I get down here at 0630 and leave at 1530. I like that.

"My worst and best experiences? My most embarrassing moment came on a yuppie commuter boat which I had backed into a mud bank, causing the engine to catch fire. Best, unequivocally, is being able to work with my family!"

Captains Chrissy and Judy, senior McDevitt now work for a former shipmate at Bay State Towing, Captain Conti Coluntino, who along with two partners, bought Russell Tripp's company and renamed it Constellation Towing and Marine, Inc. A graduate of the Massachusetts Maritime Academy, Captain Coluntino had 20 years at sea up and down the east coast of the

United States before becoming a family man and settling for harbor work in the port of Boston which enables him to be with his kids more often. Although mom Judy tries to concentrate on college and writing, the magic of tugboating is still in her blood, and she will pitch in if needed.

Both Tripp and Coluntino, and almost everyone else on the Boston waterfront, heap lavish praise on the McDeviit girls. There is enormous respect for them, and complete confidence in their tugboating skills. All are in total agreement that the McDevitt's are as good or better than anyone on the water. Captain Coluntino adds:

> *"Having them on our team—just knowing they are around—brings additional civility to a profession often known for its brusqueness. We just love them!"*

At 0400 on a gentle summer morning, I had a chance to watch the McDevitt girls in action. They had crewed up on three different Bay State Towing tugs to meet and dock an inbound tanker, the *Maersk Rochester*, bringing refined petroleum products to Boston from the Newfoundland refineries. Captain Judy, senior, was at the helm of the 3800HP twin-screw tug, *Little Joe*, now Constellation Towing's *Tucana*; daughter Chris skippered the tug *Molly*, now *Orion*; Captain Coluntino on board *Alex C*, now *Draco;* and a Reinauer boat from Boston Transportation and Towing was the fourth vessel involved in this docking. *Maersk Rochester* was headed up Chelsea Creek, which would require a sharp turn to starboard and passage through bridge openings just four feet wider than its beam. Not much room for error.

Listening to radio communications from the docking pilot to the four tugs and to the short responding blasts on their whistles, watching the deftness of movement as Judy McDevitt's hands handled *Little Joe's* throttle and steering controls, it was clear that all four tugs were under the care of experienced professionals. Gender never mattered and never should.

The McDevitt girls have certainly made their impression on the Boston waterfront. Growing up on Peddock's Island enabled them to become important east coast mariners, their nautical skills so sharply honed under their parent's guidance. The tugboat community is better because of them!

One of Michael McDevitt's tugs is aptly named the *McDevitt Girls* in honor of his mom and sisters, tugboat captains all.

Captain Arthur Surprenant

Captain Arthur Surprenant

Tugboats often seem to have personalities, almost souls, of their own. Here two of Boston Towing and Transportation Company's vessels, *Harold A. Reinauer II* and *Cornell*, seem to be having a conversation of their own as they await an inbound LNG tanker in Boston's outer harbor.

On a beautiful June day I am aboard the tug *Vincent D. Tibbetts, Jr.*, as we, along with five other boats belonging to the eleven-vessel fleet of Boston Towing and Transportation Company, scramble off the dock at 1130 to meet an incoming LNG (Liquid Natural Gas) tanker. The company, Boston's largest, is based in East Boston, across the harbor from the city itself which is showing off its dramatic skyline on this late spring morning.

Originally called Boston Fuel & Transportation, BT&T was founded in 1932 by Bert Reinauer of New York. In the early 1950s, Captain Vincent D. Tibbetts, Sr. became a partner in the company and the third generation of Reinauers, the second generation of Tibbetts are at the helm today.

This day, the *Vincent D. Tibbetts, Jr.*, a twin-screw 3,000HP boat powered by two 12-cylinder EMD diesels, is under the command of Captain Arthur Surprenant. The *Vincent*, as she is fondly known, is the company's 24-hour boat, meaning she is crewed around the clock with a captain and a mate, two AB's and one engineer. They stand watches—six hours on, six hours off—for a two-week period, and then have two weeks off before reporting back to the tug for another hitch. Unless already working, she will be the first tug dispatched by BT&T as ship assist or towing requests are received.

A half-hour ride down the harbor is Deer Island, Boston's large sewerage treatment facility. Here, we will meet the inbound tanker *Norman Lady*. The ship is a bit late, so the *Vincent* and the five other BT&T tugs—the *Maverick*, carrying the docking pilot, and the *Harold A. Reinauer II*, the *Ethel Tibbetts*, the *Cornell* and the *H. J. Reinauer*—congregate in the shipping channel. Other traffic being absent, the crews and the boats themselves seem to be able to chat with each other.

In addition to the six tugs ready to meet the inbound LNG ship, there is a flotilla of State Police and Coast Guard craft, ranging in size from small Zodiaks to cutters, and a helicopter overhead, providing security for this potentially dangerous vessel. Boston is one of the few cities in the world where the plant receiving the LNG cargo is very close to the city's center. In most other ports, the discharge terminals are located farther away from heavily populated areas. Post 9/11 security is very tight, as it should be.

We pick up *Norman Lady* "on the fly," as the tugboat crews say, and make up to her port bow as directed by the docking pilot. An hour and a half later, after the six tugs have turned her around in the upper harbor and eased her stern first under the Tobin Bridge and up the Mystic River, *Norman Lady* is secured to her pier and can begin unloading.

Vincent is dispatched to Boston's container terminal, first to undock the Mediterranean

Shipping Company's container ship *MSC INSA*, and then, almost in the same breath, to dock her incoming sister ship *MSC Claudia*. Boston harbor is an active waterway this day. While we were busy with the container ships, a Russian tanker, heavily loaded with oil, steamed in, while the *Nordeuropa*, a Swedish tanker, emptied of its precious cargo, headed out to sea.

As watches change, there is a chance to talk to the *Vincent*'s crew, beginning with Arthur Surprenant, her captain:

"I grew up in Fairhaven, Massachusetts, exposed to the sea and boats from a very early age. I did a stint in the US Coast Guard, serving on the USCG cutter Sherman, *which is where I first learned about gas turbines. After my discharge, I worked for a dock building outfit back home, using small tugs to move construction equipment around. Then I joined a marine towing company in Boston and followed that by moving to New York where I worked for Turecamo. By the time ten years had elapsed, I had earned a 500-ton captain's license and in 1992 I returned to Boston to join BT&T.*

"In those days we did a lot of offshore towing, both out of Boston and New York, and I became familiar with most of the waters along the east coast, all the way from Florida to Canada. I had what the Coast Guard calls 'recency'—in-depth knowledge of certain ports and waterways—in most of them. To get recency you have to transit the waters a dozen times within a year, inbound and outbound, both at night and during the day, under the observation of a more-experienced mariner who already has recency for that particular location or a pilot. Then you must pass USCG tests to receive their documentation. Without it, especially on petroleum barges and petrol product-carrying vessels, you cannot operate without a local pilot aboard.

"Recency is important, saving towing companies a lot of money! Once you have recency, you hold it for five years and, prior to expiration, it can be renewed by taking one round trip in those waters, again with a pilot aboard.

"Like most offshore towing crews, I have had a few experiences I could have done without. We once broke a towing hawser and parted with our tow, an oil barge, while 30

BT&T's *Vincent D. Tibbetts, Jr.,* or the *Vincent,* as she is affectionately called, moves smartly past Boston's downtown skyline, the clocked Custom House Tower dating back to the sailing days of old. *Vincent* is BT&T's 24-hour boat, always crewed up and ready. Four crew members—captain, mate, deckhand and engineer, work two weeks on, two off, and stand six hours on, six off, watches while aboard. BT&T is Boston's largest marine towing company.

miles out of Portland, Maine and 15 miles south of Monhegan Island. It was the middle of the night, of course, in a southwest wind but we were so far offshore that we had a lot of time to come back alongside the barge to retrieve her. The barge was unmanned but we were able to get the tankerman aboard to remake the tow. Unfortunately, seas had risen to more than ten feet by then and we were unable to get him off again—so he had to find shelter in one of the pump houses on a very cold winter night. By the time we neared Rockland, Maine, the weather improved and we were able to get him back on board the tug to thaw him out!

"The other excitement I can remember was while I was working with Eklof Marine in New York. We had a contract to haul a 550-foot-long New York sludge barge, 105 feet wide, drawing 38 feet of water, from Gravesend Bay to the 106-Mile Dump, which is 106 miles east of Ambrose Light. Because the sludge had to be pumped out very slowly, it took five days on site to do that job. A day's tow out and a day back meant that you had to find a seven-day weather window to do that job and that was not always easy!"

Captain Surprenant and his wife have one daughter, Jillian, of whom they are very proud. She is a graduate of the Massachusetts Maritime Academy and works for the Military Sealift Command as third assistant engineer on board the *USNS Big Horn*. Seems like dad passed his need for salt water on to his daughter!

The mate on board the *Vincent*, Robinson Lee, grew up in Harwich on fabled Cape Cod and started fishing for a living at a very young age, building his first boat in 1986.

"We fished for cod and did some trawling, but by 1989 the handwriting was on the wall regarding the fishing industry here in Massachusetts. On top of that, I never could claim to have been a very good businessman—which a commercial fisherman has to be—so I looked for a job in the towboat industry with a fairly reliable paycheck and benefits, working first for Poling Transportation and Turecamo on Staten Island, New York, and then joining BT&T in 1993.

"Most of my offshore sea experiences were on the fishing boat but, while I was sailing on the Jennifer Turecamo in New York, we would tow cement barges from Albany on the Hudson River and then down the coast to West Palm Beach in Florida. That was a pretty regular run, leaving Albany and stopping at Baltimore, Norfolk, Charleston and Jacksonville before ending at West Palm. That was especially nice in the winter, when we would leave Albany at 20 below zero and end up basking in the sun in Florida four or five days later. Not bad duty.

Rick West

Skip Lee

"I had been trying to get a Boston job for some time when, one day, we were up here on the Jennifer Turecamo *and a crewmate of mine suggested stopping at BT&T, where he knew someone who worked in the company's administration. My buddy vouched for me and suggested they hire me and a short while later they did! Still living on Cape Cod with my wife, it's nice to be able to work on the BT&T boats right here in Boston."*

Though his crewmates call him "Skip," Robinson Lee, tall and handsome with a finely chiseled face, might well have captained one of Massachusetts' world-class sailing ships back in the 1800s, had he lived at that time. He has a master's license, which allows him to tow just about anything afloat. Although this day he was working on the *Vincent*, BT&T's 24-hour boat, he also can be found in the wheelhouse of other BT&T harbor tugs from time to time. He looks and acts the part of a New England mariner and, with his shipmates, contributes much to Boston harbor.

Rick West, thirteen years with BT&T, is the engineer. He carefully checks the instrumentation on the EMD diesels every half our or so while, at the same time, making sure that there are no unusual noises or smells in the engine room. Periodic eyeball checks are done by the deck crew during times when Rick is asleep, and he is awakened if needed. Rick performs routine maintenance on the boat's engines as well and, should major work be required, *Vincent*, like her fleet mates, heads to the shipyard for repair. Because these are such rugged tugs, this type of work is not often necessary.

Rounding out this crew, which has worked together for some time now, are the two Able Bodied Seamen, Bill Wengel and Tom Guoba. Although he has a good number of marine towing years under his belt, mostly in the lumber industry in Everett, Washington, Bill is the youngest crew member on board today. He is working towards his master's license.

Tom Gouba owned a swordfish boat for fifteen years, working off the coasts of the northeastern United States and Canada—wherever the fish were feeding. His boat sank off the Grand Banks on a September voyage but, unlike the *Andrea Gail* of "The Perfect Storm," he and his crew were rescued rather quickly by a Finnish freighter in the area. He has been with BT&T for just over a year and, although he has held a master's license in commercial fishing for many years, Tom must now meet new Coast Guard requirements before he can become a captain in the marine towing industry.

We finish docking *MSC Claudia* shortly after 1700 and are sent to Salem, Massachusetts, about 20 miles up the coast to the north, to undock a coal ship that had finished unloading its cargo at the Salem power plant. She had actually been scheduled to sail earlier in the day, but the arrival of the LNG tanker had taken priority. Clouds gathered and weather reports were predicting severe thunder storms in the area as we moved up the coast at just above 11 knots. Expected at 1800, we arrived about an hour later, almost simultaneously with the weather.

The sky took on unusual colors—dark storm clouds accented by yellow and purple hues—and soon, bright lightning flashed both horizontally and vertically, illuminating broad sections of the small harbor around us. The pilot waited patiently for the weather to clear, but as darkness fell, winds became stronger. As the empty coal ship was about to head down the very narrow Salem Ship Channel, which is bordered by small islands that are difficult to see, he eventually postponed *Sophie Oldendorff*'s sailing until the next morning, and *Vincent* and her companion *Maverick* began the two-hour journey back to their East Boston home.

For the *Vincent*'s crew and for other boats in the BT&T fleet, it had been a busy day. While we were in Salem, another container ship had arrived and the *MSC Claudia*, docked earlier that afternoon, would be finished handling its containers and ready to sail by 0100 in the morning. I realized that these container ships were like UPS trucks of the sea, unloading and loading only some of their cargo in each port on their endless journeys around the world.

I had been privileged to observe crew life on board a 24-hour harbor tug. Since most global-trade products travel by ship, it is safe to say that world trade would stop if tugs were to vanish. The next time the plant where you work ships a turbine engine to Poland—or you proudly wear your new sneakers made in China—think of the mariners who crew these tugs and of the boats themselves. They are a very important part of all our lives.

Above, New York City-based Moran Towing's tug *Scott Turecamo* eases a cement barge she has been pushing towards her Boston dock. At right, deckhand, Bill Wengel, sends his heaving line up to the deck of an inbound vessel.

Captain Chris Deeley

Captain Chris Deeley

It's 0630 on the day of the summer solstice, and with an easy astern throttle, we push gently off the Boston Towing and Transportation docks in East Boston into the harbor waters. The *Jason Reinauer*, twin-screws and 2,000HP, is under the command of Captain Chris Deeley. Our engineer is Tim Machaiek and on deck is the AB, Charlie Gibbons.

Our first heading is toward Boston's container terminal in the Reserve Channel, where we pick up the docking pilot, Dave Galman. The long pier is empty at the moment but will soon receive two container ships, each over 900 feet in length. In the outer harbor, just out of the North Channel, is the *Weser Bridge*, of German registry from Bremen, currently under charter to a Chinese shipping company. She is high out of the water indicating a light load, her bulbous bow protruding, moving at a good clip as we come up along her starboard side to put the docking pilot aboard. He will take command of the ship from the sea pilot who has brought her in this far.

Throttling back, Chris lets *Weser Bridge* overtake the tug until we are near her starboard stern. Charlie and Tim are on the bow, ready to make up to the container ship with a ship's line placed over a "Panama Chock," recessed into the freighter's hull at tug level. The chock has been designed for this position for times like today, when the freighter is riding high out of the water. Under this condition, a line fastened to a chock on deck might create dangerous tensions for the tug that could lead to its capsizing, one of the greatest dangers in the tugboat industry.

Once secure, with *Harold A. Reinauer, II* on the port bow, the pilot's command for "full ahead" results in all 2,000 of *Jason Reinauer*'s horses pushing hard to turn *Weser Bridge* in preparation for her stern-first approach to the container pier. The docking is occurring on an incoming flood tide, which means that the pilot does not have to allow for a lot of leeway between ship and dock as he would if the tide were ebb. Under those conditions, we would now be much farther up the harbor, expecting the tide to help push the large vessel back down harbor against its dock.

At just the precise time and on the pilot's order, *Jason Reinauer* releases her line and sneaks under the freighter's stern to make up to her port side for the final push to the dock. The whole operation, from when we first picked up *Weser Bridge* inbound, until her docking lines are secure, has taken less than an hour. *Jason Reinauer*'s crew has done this often and their professionalism, and that of the docking pilot, shows.

BT&T's recent fleet additions were former Navy tugs called YTB's (Yard Tugboats). Here the *Vincent* shifts one of the former YTB's so her port side can face the dock and her fendering can be completed. BT&T has also received two tractor tugs built in Boothbay Harbor, Maine. They add a great deal of power to the BT&T fleet.

Captain Deeley has been on tugboats for 14 years, including seven with Eklof Towing in New York, five with Bay State Towing in Boston and two with BT&T. There was a three-year respite for work as a New England harbormaster in both Gloucester and Beverly, Massachusetts. He is now studying for his Boston pilot's license and hopes to receive it within two years.

AB Gibbons has captained several commuter and tourist boats in Boston's harbor and has operated his own lobster boat in the same waters for more than 20 years. He also sailed on one of BT&T's coastal tankers that used to supply fuel to the islands off Massachusetts, like Nantucket, before the power plant there made a direct underwater pipeline connection to the mainland and fuel delivery by sea was no longer needed. Now he is a tugboat deckhand and likes it that way. Tim, the engineer, has more than three years at the Massachusetts Maritime Academy behind him as well as a good amount of sea time out of Portsmouth, New Hampshire, working on vessels that used to supply the Russian factory ships with herring and other fish species of which some Americans are not too fond. Tim has also worked overseas on an offshore drilling ship.

With the *Weser Bridge* docking complete, we move back into the harbor and quickly see the next container ship, *MSC INSA*, approaching. She is a Mediterranean Shipping Company vessel that had sailed from Boston just ten days before. Now she was on her way back up the east coast, calling in such ports as Baltimore and New York. Later, she will head east across the Atlantic to her first European port of call.

MSC INSA is much more heavily loaded and, therefore, much lower in the water. So low, in fact, that her propellers are stirring up a lot of debris from the harbor's floor, quite visible in the water beneath us. She is drawing about 42 feet of water and the docking pilot has to be acutely aware of these conditions. The shipping channel's depth is not the same shore to shore and, occasionally, ships do scrape the bottom— some even run aground. But not today. *MSC INSA* slips slowly astern and, ever so carefully, towards her dock. The first container is off the ship just as the last docking line is secure. By day's end, both these vessels will be at sea again. The days when sailors used to have a "girl in every port" are over. These crews get substantial time off only when their relief comes aboard.

By 1015 we are back at BT&T's home base. The first jobs on this ten-hour day for *Jason Reinauer*'s crew are complete and there is time for their breakfast before she will leave the dock again. On the dock, I meet *Harold A. Reinauer, II*'s skipper, Captain Bill Potter, and deckhand, Jim Nelson.

Potter has been with BT&T for 13 years. He comes from a family of mariners and his grandfather also worked on tugs in Boston Harbor. Four years of Navy time placed him on FFG's (Guided Missile Frigates). His worst times? Running petroleum barges from Boston to Bangor, Maine while Nor'easters churned the sea to uncomfortable heights, producing the offshore tugboat's least-liked weather conditions.

Captain Potter's deckhand, Jim Nelson, started out as an oiler on tugs 33 years ago (when there were such jobs).

"In those days a tug crew would consist of a captain, mate, deckhand, cook, engineer and oiler. The oiler was an assistant to the engineer, wiping down the engines and everything else in the engine room. Today those crew sizes have been cut in half and, on some harbor boats, you will find only a captain and a 'deckineer'.

"I used to do a lot of offshore work hauling barges, mostly loaded with petrol, south to Rhode Island and New York, north to New Hampshire and Maine. But I think my greatest tugboat memory here in Boston was when the tall ships came in for the first time, in 1976. That was an incredible day! My worst time? Probably a voyage on the tanker Gulf Tiger *in the North Atlantic bringing a load of jet fuel to Rotterdam during winter storms, running into mountainous seas that ran higher than the stack of the ship. She was a MSTS (Military Sea Transport Ship) vessel."*

I leave Jim Nelson on the dock splicing a ship line and head for some breakfast as well.

(top) Captain Bill Potter
(bottom) Jim Nelson

Captain George Grimes

Captain George Grimes

Captain George Grimes owned his first row boat at the age of seven, and by the time he was a teenager, he worked as a deck hand on a gaff-rigged ketch named *Scylla* taking tourists from the harbor in Rockport, Massachusetts to the waters of nearby Sandy Bay. If any further reinforcement was needed to push George towards a maritime career, he found it during active experience with the Rockport Sea Scouts. His Rockport High School yearbook picture caption predicted that he would make his living on the sea. Four years later, after graduating from the Maine Maritime Academy, the prediction came true as Third Officer George Grimes reported for duty on board the break-bulk freighter *Exminster* docked in Hoboken, New Jersey.

"The term 'break-bulk freighter' probably doesn't mean much in today's maritime world where container ships, oil tankers and bulk carriers make up the majority of the ocean going cargo fleet. But forty years ago, these ships were really the dominant vessels. American Export-Isbrandtsen Lines, owner of the Exminster, *was typical of the ocean freight lines of that time. The freighter that I boarded just out of the Academy was a typical ship of that time—superstructure and stack amidships, with three to four cargo hatches forward and aft. These vessels were equipped with many booms, used to load and unload the ship's varied cargo.* Exminster *actually had 27 of these cargo booms.*

"I left Castine, Maine after graduating from the Maine Maritime Academy on a Friday, reported for duty the next Monday and four and a half months later, at age 21, completed my first trip around the world. I stayed with the company for six years until I met my wife, Sally, and decided to come ashore for a while to pursue our relationship. It was a wise decision, resulting in a very happy 30-year marriage, two beautiful daughters and a dog named Gretel."

Often a sailor is a sailor, even ashore, and so George started a number of marine-related shore assignments including jobs at the yacht club in Manchester-by-the-Sea and the Landmark School just down the road. There Grimes created a new sailing program around General George S. Patton's schooner, the *When and If*. The Patton family had donated her to the school which was seeking a permanent captain for the boat.

"We used to sail down the coast of Maine with two teachers, myself and ten kids aboard. It was an excellent program which became quite popular at the school, keeping me busy for four years. But the urge to go back to sea and raise my license in grade—I was second mate at the time and wanted to become a captain—was strong and so I joined the Atlantic Richfield fleet of supertankers sailing on the US west coast between Long Beach, CA, Panama and Valdez, Alaska. By 1982 I had become a licensed master though most of my work aboard the tankers was as chief officer."

By 1991 Captain Grimes went shoreside again to stay closer to his family. He became an "expediter and loss control specialist".

"An expediter in the maritime industry is a person who verifies the measurements of cargo. If a company sends an oil tanker down to Venezuela, for instance, as is often the case, they want to be sure that when the vessel is loaded all the oil that is supposed to be aboard has actually come aboard. These duties are usually done best by personnel who are familiar with that type of vessel. My many years of experience shipping on oil tankers certainly gave me that credibility. Other people specialize in various bulk cargoes, such as grain or ore—it just depends on which ships you know the best. At times there can be as many as three people all watching the cargo-measurement process. One might be representing the terminal, one the ship owner and one the group that owns the cargo! The job itself, as it turned out, was even worse than being away at sea for stretches at a time

because you were always on call. Sea time away was at least fairly predictable while working as an expediter you never really knew when you might have to leave again on very short notice.

"I knew that I had to make another career change, so I became a teacher, going back to college for the required educational courses and then teaching 100 students at Marstons Mills Middle School on Cape Cod. Though I am somewhat disappointed to say it, I was a teacher for less than five months. I was never really sure whether it was the approximately ten percent of the students who constantly disrupted the class or whether it was the subject matter I was teaching which caused me to submit my resignation. At any rate, I came home one day and went for a walk with Gretel, my golden retriever. When we returned to the house I informed my wife that Gretel and I had just had a long conversation discussing my teaching future and that Gretel thought I ought to resign. The sea beckoned yet again. This time I followed a long time dream of becoming a tugboat captain."

To do that, George Grimes, holder of a master's license which would have qualified him to serve on many an ocean-going vessel and a man now in his fifties, had to start all over again as a deckhand on a tugboat. Hearing his wife say that "you should follow your dream" and knowing that she was supportive of him, he started working for Maritrans, Inc. in Puerto Rico on a tugboat named *Declaration*.

"I started out as an AB/Tankerman—that is, an able bodied seaman who specializes in the petroleum industry. That meant that, when the tugboat was under way alone, I was a deckhand, and when the barge was being discharged or loaded, I was a tankerman, in charge of the 60,000-barrel cargo of black oil. By August, 2001, after two years as an AB/ tankerman and two years of training as a mate, I was able to become a qualified tugboat captain. Through a twist of fate, I ended up with my first captain's assignment on board the same tug on which I had started as a deckhand years earlier.

Constellation Towing and Marine's tug *Tucana* departs its home dock. Formerly Bay State Towing's *Little Joe*, she is one of Boston's hardest working tugboats.

A fleet of BT&T tugs returns to home base after completing a docking ship-assist job for an inbound tanker. Boston's Tobin Bridge is in the background.

"The company I now work for has three tugs and three petroleum barges in Puerto Rico Our runs are quite regular from Guayanilla on the southwest coast near Ponce, to a small oil terminal in Aguirre. Dock to dock it is roughly a nine-hour run. The oil comes to Guayanilla in tankers, mostly from Venezuela, and is off-loaded there into an oil storage facility. There used to be a sugar factory in Aguirre but now it is just a very sleepy little place with a power plant that needs a barge-full of oil every two days in order to generate electricity for the Puerto Rican government. We usually make the barge up on our side and tow it 'on the hip', until we're on open ocean. Then we let out the wire, which is already attached to the towing bridle, until we approach the destination.

"The barges measure 350 by 60 feet and draw only three feet of water when they're empty, nineteen and a half feet when they are full. The toughest part of the boat-handling job usually comes in restricted waters with the wind and current affecting the barge's course adversely. The channel in Aguirre is quite narrow and requires careful navigation. The Declaration, operated by Energy Services Puerto Rico, Inc., is now named the Caribe Service. The parent company, Hornbeck Offshore, has a large fleet of barges and tugs, some operating out of Brooklyn, New York. But I like it down in Puerto Rico where the atmosphere is more 'laid back' as opposed to New York where it is much more stressful and busy. The traffic in the New York area is so much heavier and the need for control so much greater, that working barges up and down the East River or the Hudson River can be quite a challenge."

The rotation routine—three weeks on duty in Puerto Rico and three weeks off back home—seems to work well for Captain Grimes and his family. At the time of our interview, his two daughters were doing well, one in a Master's program at Boston College and one a junior at

Merrimack College. His cooking skills, honed to near-perfection during his three-week stints in Puerto Rico where he takes his turn at the griddle along with the other crew members, come in very handy while he is home since his wife is frequently busy as an educational consultant.

With a lifelong career at sea measuring 37 years, (minus a few interruptions ashore), Captain Grimes shares some of his more memorable career experiences:

"We were on board the Exminster *in Kobe, Japan, off-loading a cargo of tea packed in small plywood crates which had been loaded in Hong Kong. The crates were all stacked in the 'tween decks and in order to get to the lower holds of the ship we had to take all the shoring out of the 'tween deck areas. In the middle of the night, on my watch, we received orders from the harbormaster to sail because of the threat of an impending typhoon. When I passed the message on to the captain, he said he was not about to move his ship. A few hours later we received a similar but even more urgent message, again ordering us to sail, which the captain again ignored. An hour later we saw automobile headlights coming down the dock, which turned out to be the pilot who came aboard saying 'we're letting the lines go whether you like it or not—you must sail.' By now, of course, the captain was in a big panic."*

'Chief, we have to warm up the engines and get going'
'Captain, we don't have time to get the hatch boards back in.'
'Never mind the hatch boards, we have to set sail.'

"So off we go into the area just outside Kobe harbor, which is an enclosed bay about 20 miles square. The winds by now are blowing at 120 miles an hour, visibility is zero, the ship is underway because the captain has chosen not to anchor due to a problem with the anchor windlass. We are literally dodging those vessels that are anchored because we really can't see them until the last moment. Exminster *is rocking so severely that the lookout slides from one end of the bridge to the other, smashing his head and falling unconscious. The cook comes up from the galley complaining about the conditions and is ordered off the bridge by the captain. And all the Hong Kong tea that is now fairly unprotected between-decks is sloshing around in the holds making a pretty unpleasant sight!*

"My supertanker days spawned a few choice experiences also. You leave Valdez, fully loaded with 1.8 million barrels of oil on a ship that is 980 feet long, down so low in the water that your draft is 59 feet. Then you hit the open Pacific with your bow splitting the oncoming waves and, as heavy as you are, the ship feels like it is climbing uphill on each one. And it was even rougher heading north under ballast because the winds were usually out of the southwest on the beam, causing the tanker to roll constantly from side to side. My wife came along on one of the trips and we were rolling so badly that she asked if we were all right. When I replied that I thought so, she said: 'What do you mean, you think so—you work on this boat!' But, all in all, I was fortunate to have survived those voyages and to have experienced that era of the shipping industry. Many of those types of ships, like the break bulkers, no longer exist, having been replaced by container ships."

A tugboat captain now, George Grimes will probably keep working as long as his employer is confident he can still climb the ladders necessary to do the job, and can still stand the watches that are required to move that oil to where it's needed. Chances are that will be for quite a long time.

Erie Canal Tow

Captain Joe Simpson

Captain Joe Simpson

Standing on the shore of New York's Lake Oneida on a gray and occasionally wet summer afternoon, I stared westward towards the horizon, waiting for the Simpson Towing Company tug *Chaplain* to appear. She had left St. Catherines, Ontario, Canada, the morning of the day before, bound for Boston with a cargo of two Canadian-built boilers securely lashed by cables to the 200-foot barge she was pushing. Like a sailor marooned on a distant shore, I was wishing for the tug to come when, suddenly, Sylvan Beach's gray skies parted like the Red Sea, creating a dramatic red-ball sunset just as *Chaplain* and tow broke over the horizon.

By 2100, barge and tug were secure to the embankment and my gear was stowed aboard next to my fo'c'sle bunk. I had met *Chaplain*'s captain, Joe Simpson, on an earlier Boston ship-docking job and now was introduced to brother and First Mate Pete Simpson (who also has a captain's license and is a corporate pilot when not tugboating). Also on board is nephew Bob Wallace, the AB/deckhand, and Joe's father, Jim, partner in the company and an experienced tugboat captain himself. Jim is designated the chief maintenance officer for this trip. It's a family affair.

By 2300, after having a meal on the beach, I was sound asleep. At 0730 next morning, *Chaplain* slipped its lines and headed east on the Erie Canal towards lock 22. Over the next two days, 21 more would follow along a route through the Mohawk Valley which transits through some of the most historic parts of the northeastern United States. George Washington and his troops fought many battles in the area, including the Battle of Saratoga, just northeast of the canal's beginning, which became the turning point of the Revolutionary War.

When the Erie Canal was opened on October 26th, 1825, it was the engineering wonder of its day. Including its tributary canal systems—Oswego, Champlain and Cayuga-Seneca—it contains a total of 57 locks, with lifts that range from 6 to 40.5 feet, raising the canal from tide-water level at Troy to a height of 572 feet where it meets the Niagra River, 338 miles to the west. In the beginning, it had a depth of four feet and a width of forty. Today, controlling

The tug *Chaplain*, built in Brooklyn, New York, for work on the Erie Canal and the rivers surrounding New York City, has a pilot house that can move up and down on pistons within an eight-foot range. Lowered, *Chaplain* is able to clear low bridges in the area while a fully raised wheelhouse provides good visibility over loaded barges she might be pushing. Here she is leaving one of the 22 locks on the Erie Canal which she and her tow will have to transit on their voyage from St. Catherine's, Ontario, Canada, to Boston, Massachusetts.

vary from 12 to 14 feet and the locks themselves are 42.5 feet wide with massive steel doors at either end, some weighing as much as 200,000 pounds!

As heavy as they are, they can be opened and closed in about 30 seconds and the entire passage through a lock takes an average of 20 minutes. The Erie Canal is ten times as long as the Panama Canal, and has approximately four times the lift and just short of ten times as many locks. Designed and built almost a century before the canal crossing Panama, the Erie Canal was an enormous engineering feat of its time.

In the early days, the Erie Canal brought coal and grain to the east and took American settlers west, spawning the growth of cities like Amsterdam, Utica, Syracuse and Buffalo along its route. Soon after the canal opened, New York City replaced Philadelphia as the nation's principal seaport.

Even though domestic waterborne commercial tonnage in the United States still comes close to the foreign import/export figures (1 billion tons compared to 1.4 billion tons according to the US Army Corps of Engineers Navigation Data Center statistics for the year 2000), the once-frenzied pace of barge traffic on the Erie Canal has subsided for many reasons. The New York State Thruway, which parallels the canal in many places, allows trucks to move much of the product that was once barged on the Erie; petroleum that once traveled on fuel barges now flows through northeast pipelines. Today, the Erie Canal mostly serves the recreational boating community.

Which is why, when a barge tow does come through, lock tenders and visitors alike express curiosity and enthusiasm to the crew. So much so that the words "Boilers to Boston and

The tug *Mary Alice* moves quickly past us as she heads east on Long Island Sound towards Boston. There she will pick up a crane barge and tow it south to New York City at a considerably slower speed.

Maryland," written in bold letters on the side of the equipment just after we had transited our second lock, provided a quick and easy answer to the most frequently asked question!

Expert boat handler Joe Simpson displayed his artistry at each of the 22 locks through which we passed. Guiding an 85-foot-long tugboat and its tow, a 200 x 40-foot barge, into locks that measure 300 x 42.5 feet proved to be quite a challenge every time. There is little clearance fore or aft, as room must be left for the lock's doors as they swing inward towards the vessel when the raising or lowering of the water level has been completed. You sure can't put the tug on automatic pilot. Positioned on the bow of the barge, two-way radios in hand, AB Wallace and First Mate Pete Simpson helped by letting Joe know when he needed to nudge the barge to the left or right.

We ran the Erie for 18 hours that first day, giving me a chance to get to know *Chaplain*, and finally reaching Amsterdam, where, by 0100, we tied up for the night. She is an attractive old timer, by vessel standards, built in Brooklyn, New York, in 1952. Named for the four chaplains who lost their lives when they gave their life vests to shipmates after being sunk in the North Atlantic during World War II, she too seems courageous. Single-screw and driven by a 12-cylinder 1500HP diesel, she is a workhorse!

Built for New York harbor and its fixed bridges and fairly shallow waters, she is well suited for her role as a "canaller." Her pilot house moves up and down on pistons, providing an eight-foot range for high visibility over or around loads like the boilers, as well as low 15-foot clearances when needed. Three sister tugs, the *Crow*, *Cheyenne* and *Choctaw*, were all built the same way. All but *Choctaw* are still working.

By 1800 of day two, we reached Waterford, New York, where the Erie Canal had its beginning. This is where the Mohawk River, which the Erie uses for much of its water in the canal's current, modern version, has its confluence with the mighty Hudson River. Here, the crew took a well-earned three-hour restaurant break before a 2100 departure. The Federal lock in Troy, New York, is the last one heading south, and by 2230 we reached the open river and began a serious all-night sprint for New York City. Because the Hudson is tidal, this passage can take 13 to 20 hours, depending on how much flood tide is encountered. Knowledge of tides and tide charts becomes critical to mariners as they plan their approaches to New York City; it is not important on the Erie Canal since there are no tides.

Lady Luck rode with us that night as we sped by Albany, brightly lit for its nocturnal outreach. Before daylight, we had passed the cities of Ravena, Hudson, Kingston and Poughkeepsie. There is even a small community called Cementon, which, appropriately, produces a lot of cement. Though the Hudson is deep-draft navigable north as far as Albany, we saw no signs of ocean-going vessels either in port or on the river. Spending a good bit of time with Captain Joe during his midnight to 0600 watch, I was impressed by the many navigational aids on the Hudson, clearly marking the channels for mariners as they travel—larger beacons flashing their reds and greens in contrast to the smaller buoys with only reflective colors in place on the Erie Canal. There are even beacons on which a vessel can line up its bow or stern to achieve the proper course at night. When aligned correctly, the light will be white, and as ships or boats move off course to starboard or port, shades of red will begin to be seen.

The computer charts most mariners use for navigation these days are amazingly detailed, with overhead obstructions such as bridges and power lines clearly marked—critical knowledge

AB Bob Wallace removes a ship's line from a chock inside a lock on the Erie Canal. Tows are secured inside the lock in this manner, making sure that tug and barge are not in the way of the lock's doors as they swing inward once the water levels have been raised or lowered.

for the skipper towing tall cargoes such as our boilers. Paper charts are still required for back-up. Because the display is interfaced with the GPS (Global Positioning System), the screen on the captain's laptop includes an icon showing *Chaplain*'s position at all times.

As dawn broke on my third day aboard *Chaplain*, we were just north of the Newburgh Bridge which spans the Hudson. West Point, in all its glory, loomed to starboard not long after and as we passed "The Point" I could almost hear General Douglas McArthur's deep voice giving his famous "duty, honor, country" speech in the Academy's cafeteria. By noontime we were in sight of the George Washington Bridge which, many years ago, I had crossed on foot with my then 80-year-old grandmother. She was like that.

A flood tide was beginning to flow up river against us so Captain Simpson decided to turn left into the Harlem River, under the Spuyten Duyvil Bridge. Avoiding having to navigate down the Hudson, past lower Manhattan where the World Trade Center towers once proudly stood, would save three hours and considerable fuel on this extremely hot, 100+ degree, New York summer day.

We passed through Hell's Gate without difficulty and soon were abreast of Laguardia Airport, then under the Whitestone Bridge and on Long Island Sound with approximately 24 hours of running left. With the toughest navigational challenges now behind him, Joe could put *Chaplain* on automatic pilot, plotting a course almost due east from the beginning of Long Island Sound eastward to the western entrance of the Cape Cod Canal.

You could see and feel the changes in skipper and crew once they faced open and familiar waters ahead. Decks were scrubbed, the galley cleaned and a meal prepared on the *Chaplain*'s grill. By 2030 hours, with all those activities behind us, *Chaplain*'s wake, ignited by the setting sun, played out astern and the only remaining question, absent any unforeseen difficulties with tug or barge, was whether the seas would remain calm enough to continue pushing the tow.

The tug *Coral Sea*, westbound on Long Island Sound, pulling a fuel barge behind it. One billion tons of domestic waterborne cargo are shipped on America's waterways annually—almost as much tonnage as is imported from or exported abroad.

"When seas start running more than two to three feet, we need to go 'on the hawser' and start pulling the barge because the up-and-down movement of the bow of the tug on the stern of the barge becomes too great. Whenever possible, we prepare for that ahead of time by setting up the bridle and hawser gear on our aft deck. Then we just have to release the facing wires that have kept the tug's bow close and true to the barge and bring the tug around in front of the barge's bow. We try to do all that before the sea change actually occurs, having been informed either through weather faxes or other reports or simply by listening to radio transmissions of marine traffic ahead of us. We don't like to wait too long and have to transfer crew to or from the barge tow in rising seas. On the other hand, we prefer pushing to pulling because we get an extra knot per hour that way, which affects fuel costs as well as the length of the voyage."

So spoke the captain. But again luck was with us and we were able to push all the way.

A few hours of bunk time after a great meal and I was in the wheelhouse again. This would be my last night at sea and I wanted to experience it to the fullest, noting the navigational signals, the sparkle of the lights on either shore, the westbound tanker heading for New Haven, the twinkle of the stars and, not least, an ocean sunrise I had not seen since the Atlantic had beat me up on a deep-sea sail from Massachusetts to Bermuda many years before.

By 0400 we were at "The Race," a spot at sea where Long Island Sound meets the Atlantic Ocean. Marked by two red and green beacons, placed several miles apart, it is a junction that is often quite rough. But tonight, the only discernible difference between these two bodies of water was an increase in the size of the swells as we hit more-open ocean.

The only real drama the night provided was several hours of radio transmissions between a southern fishing vessel, *Miss Amanda*, which had sailed from New Bedford that evening, and the US Coast Guard. Unfamiliar with local waters, the ship had hit rocks off of Block Island and was severely damaged and in danger of sinking. The USCG was able to send boats with pumps that kept *Miss Amanda* afloat until the tug *Otter* could come to her aid.

Sunrise through a summer haze occurred precisely at 0550, just as predicted. By 1400 we had passed through the Cape Cod Canal and, six hours later, after traveling almost 500 miles with the *Chaplain*'s crew, we were tied up in Boston. Two days later they would be at sea again, pushing southward to deliver their second boiler to its Maryland home. They didn't know what would find *Chaplain*'s bow or hawser next—only that they would deliver it safely and on time.

Chaplain and tow tied up for a shoreside meal in Waterford, New York, before beginning its sprint south on the Hudson River to New York City. Here the Erie Canal had its beginning, where the Mohawk River has its confluence with the Hudson River. The Erie Canal was completed in October, 1825 and changed the face of America by opening up its western frontiers. Its completion took the title of busiest US seaport away from Philadelphia and gave it to New York.

Chaplain pushes its cargo, two huge Canadian-built boilers, down the Hudson River, past West Point and under an Interstate Highway bridge. The next day, after transiting Long Island Sound, *Chaplain* approaches the western end of the Cape Cod Canal and its raised railroad bridge in Bourne.

New York, New York

McAllister Towing and Transportation, Inc. and Moran Towing Corporation have long been known as New York City's "Irish Navy". Together with the Reinauer Corporation, the three tugboat companies handle the great majority of marine towing in the Port of New York. Ranked third by tonnage handled in US seaports, the Port of New York is always alive with vessel traffic. Cedric Bouyea, (right) a native of Guyana, works for McAllister as an AB on board the tug *Resolute*. A mariner all his life, he was a part of Guyana's Department of Marine Transport, helping his country export its products of coffee, sugar, rice, timber and bauxite.

Philadelphia, Pennsylvania

At right, *Iona McAllister* at the fuel dock. For more than 300 years, Philadelphia has been a great port city and a center for international commerce. Measured by tonnage handled, it is still one of the United States' top 20 seaports.

McAllister's Philadelphia operation includes a US Navy contract for the ship assist work in the Philadelphia Navy Yard, home to a large reserve fleet of vessels that are maintained for use should they be needed on the high seas again.

Wilmington, Delaware

Wilmington Tug's *Tina* (below), built in 1977, is reported to be the first tug in North America and the first US commercial vessel to use the then-new technology known as "Azimuthing Stern Drives." Today's state-of-the-art tugs with their ASD's forward of amidships (and sometimes aft) are commonly known as "Z-drive" or "Tractor Tugs." *Chris* (right), named after the Christina River, was Wilmington Tug's first vessel when Captain Harry Rowland, Sr., founded the company in 1965. Below, vessels carrying fruit from Central and South America call at the Port of Wilmington weekly. The refrigerated containers are transferred immediately to trucks that carry them to their final destinations.

Above, Wilmington Tug's newest tractor tug, the *Captain Harry*, joined the fleet in December, 2001. Named for the company's founder and the father of the current company president, H. Hickman Rowland, Jr., the new tug is, in "Hick's" words: "a state-of-the-art ship assist machine, perfectly suited for docking large crude oil tankers and cargo ships on the Delaware River."

Baltimore, Maryland

Paul P. Swensen is the Division Vice President and General Manager of Moran Towing of Maryland, based in the Fells Point section of Baltimore. It has been 27 years since he served on a tugboat crew, which is when he began his on-shore tug career as a dispatcher.

Paul knows the tugboat business as well as anyone, supervising five full-time crews that operate Moran Towing of Maryland's four tugs: *Cape Romain, Harriet Moran, Sewells Point* and *Cavalier.*

"We handle, on average, three to four ships a day that call in Baltimore, which tend to be RoRo vessels (roll on, roll off), container ships, bulk carriers and car ships. In addition, we move barges loaded with cement, mostly from the Hudson River Valley, or coal coming north from Norfolk. The fleet here stays pretty busy!"

Assigned to ride along on the *Cape Romain*, a twin-screw 3300HP tugboat built in 1979 and skippered this day by Captain Wesley Southworth, we move purposefully out into the channel, heading towards the Francis Scott Key bridge, where we await the arrival of the Saudi Arabian RoRo container ship *Saudi Hofuf* southbound from Philadelphia through the Chesapeake and Delaware Canal. Just off our port bow is a red, white and blue buoy marking the spot where Francis Scott Key wrote our national anthem aboard a British vessel as Fort McHenry—the famous national landmark well off to port now—was being bombarded. The waters we are on have great historical significance.

Captain Southworth is a son of the Chesapeake, having grown up in a family marina down the Bay a bit. He earned his master's license at age 27 and has been a mariner ever since—always with tugs except for a seven-year departure for work on chemical barges. His resumé

AB David Green on board Moran Towing of Maryland's *Cape Romain* wraps a ship's line around the tug's H-bitt while docking the incoming container ship *Saudi Hofuf*. A lifelong mariner, Green believes that "the sea picks you—you don't pick it."

includes five and a half years with the US Coast Guard, with stations in Point Judith, Rhode Island, and Cordova and Valdez, Alaska. Like most tugboat skippers, he loves his work.

Not quite so for the mate, Leon Mach. His father worked on tugs for more than 30 years and Leon himself has had a long career on the boats but "this is where it stops." He is not anxious for his son to follow in his footsteps.

The first ship to appear on the horizon, moving gently up the Bay, is the car carrier *Pearl Ray*, a Monrovia flagged vessel. But soon, *Saudi Hofuf* pokes its bow out from behind the land mass hiding it, and turns sharply to starboard on its path to meet us. Another Moran tug, the *Sewells Point*, which has been waiting with us, prepares to make up to the container ship's stern while we head for its port bow.

Deckhand David Green, two and a half years with Moran but a lifelong mariner, prepares to handle the lines needed for this ship-assist work. He has worked aboard cable ships, bulk carriers, container ships, oil supply vessels and now tugs and seriously believes that "the sea picks you—you don't pick it!" A graduate of both the Massachusetts Maritime Academy and the academy run by the SIU (Seafarers International Union), he feels best when he is on the water.

"Some guys cry for home after a month. My longest sea voyage was for nine months and I would have gladly stayed for nine more if the mission hadn't ended."

An hour after coming alongside *Saudi Hofuf,* she is in her berth and we make a beeline for the car ship *Pearl Ray,* which has now proceeded to a point just off her dock. Baltimore can be an extremely windy port, with wind directions being mostly out of the northwest. Sometimes,

Patricia Moran, a 4,000HP twin-screw Z-drive tug assisting an inbound container ship. More than 15,000 containers arrive at US ports daily. Baltimore's port is consistently among the nation's top 20 in terms of tonnage handled.

as is the case today, tugs are placed exactly at the vessel's bow, rather than to the side at the port or starboard bows, to be able to change the ship's direction more quickly if required to do so. Wes Southworth:

> *"These car ships, with their extremely tall superstructures, present a very large surface to the winds. It's almost like they were a sailboat with excessive sail out in heavy winds....they can easily take you where you do not want to go. So docking the car ships, especially here in Baltimore, is often a real challenge!"*

Because of the enormous heights of the sides of these vessels—which make it impractical and unwise to try to get lines from the tugs to the deck—the car ships have "Panama Chocks" built into them that are more-or-less at the same level as the deck of the tug. Still, placing the lines around them is not easy, so difficult, in fact, that David Green considers this the most dangerous part of his job.

But on this day he gets it done (as he always does), Captain Wes cooperating with some expert boat handling.

Pearl Ray is backed into her berth, which will make her departure, probably later this evening, an easier operation.

Moran Towing, founded in New York in 1860, together with McAllister Towing, is known as "the Irish Navy." Moran does a good job in Baltimore under Paul Swensen's command. As their brochure states, "the white 'M' insignia, displayed on their tug's stacks, is a fixture in ports all along the United States' eastern and Gulf coasts, from Maine to Texas."

It is a familiar symbol for a long history of leadership in the maritime towing industry.

The container ship *Saudi Hofuf* docking at her pier. Moran Towing's tug *Sewells' Point* is keeping her close to the dock while the docking lines are being *set. Saudi Hofuf* has a unique RoRo configuration as well. Just ahead is a car ship unloading. Because of the frequent high winds in Baltimore's harbor, the car ships with their very tall profiles are often difficult to dock. Both vessels will be outbound again by day's end.

Above, one of two new tractor tugs built for McAllister Towing & Transportation in 2001, the *Vicki M. McAllister* moves smartly up the Delaware River in Philadelphia. Rated at 5,000HP and 96 feet long, the *Vicki M.* can sometimes be seen working the waters of Baltimore's harbor and the Chesapeake Bay as well. At right, Moran Towing of Maryland's home in the Fells Point area of Baltimore. Four tugs: *Cape Romain, Harriet Moran, Sewells Point* and *Cavalier* handle an average of three to four ships a day, mostly RoRo vessels, container ships, bulk and car carriers. In addition, barges filled primarily with coal or cement also need Moran's attention.

Wilmington, North Carolina

Below, Navy supply vessels of the reserve fleet await another call. Cape Fear Towing Company's *Fort Caswell*, (right) ready for its next assignment. *Reid McAllister* and *Barbara McAllister* (bottom), 3600HP and 2400HP boats respectively

Barbara McAllister (opposite, top) heads to the fuel dock; (opposite bottom) dredging a channel in Charleston, South Carolina.

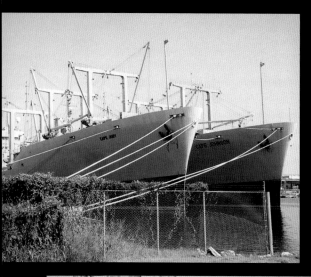

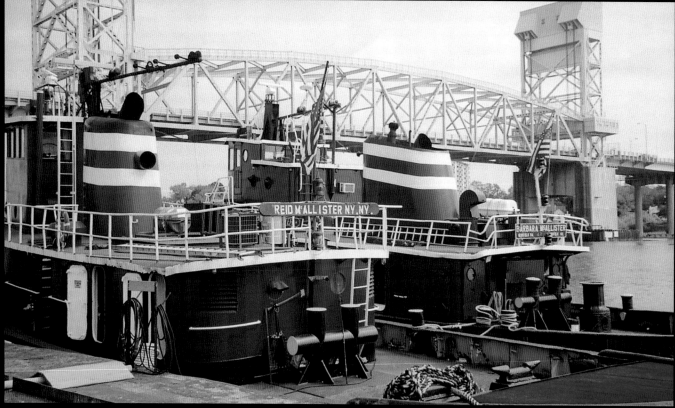

Charleston, South Carolina

Docking pilot Steve Browder (right) on the *Madison Maersk*'s automated Jacobs ladder which raises and lowers under electric power with the pilot on board. In addition to saving the pilot a considerable number of steps, the ladder is kept close in to the ship, reducing dangerous swinging, especially in higher seas. Below, the container ship *Madison Maersk* at one of the Port of Charleston's major container terminals on the Wando River.

Missy McAllister (opposite top) at work near a naval vessel. A bulk carrier (opposite bottom) moves slowly up the Cooper River with assistance from a Moran tug. A new span for the Cooper River bridges in the background is being built. When completed, it will be the longest cable-stayed bridge in the Western Hemisphere with piers twice as high as the existing ones and minimum clearances raised to 187 feet from the current height to accommodate ever-larger and taller vessels.

Above, Captain Jerry Skelton and docking pilot Steve Browder aboard McAllister's *Lewis G. Seabrook* in Charleston, South Carolina. They are awaiting the arrival of the container ship *Madison Maersk*, pictured below.

USNS Bob Hope, (opposite) a naval reserve supply ship recently returned to active duty. Several Charleston-based Moran tugs are shown at their dock.

Savannah, Georgia

Luis M. Pereira is Moran Towing of Savannah's Division Vice President and General Manager. *Cynthia Turecamo* and *Philip Turecamo* are at their Savannah dock on a raw and rainy day. *Robert Turecamo* and their new tractor tug, *Diane Moran*, are away on duty. The Port of Savannah is situated 24 miles up the Savannah River from the Atlantic Ocean. It takes the average deep-draft vessel three and a half hours to cover that distance.

Green Cove Springs, Florida

Smith Maritime engineer Alan Blun (right) trouble shooting some wiring on board the company's new tug, *Rhea*, scheduled to leave for sea trials and its first assignment just two days after this picture was taken. Below, a former Canadian Coast Guard ship in port for refitting.

Above, Smith Maritime's first tug, *Elsbeth* was built by Captain Latham Smith and Mate, Peter Newe. Newe (right) is a former German schooner captain who had built many wooden boats. *Elsbeth* was named for Latham Smith's wife. For many years the tug was home to the Smith family, including their five children, as she roamed the world. Many a birthday was celebrated in her wheelhouse. Placed into service in 1969, which included long-range towing and salvage work, *Elsbeth* has compiled an admirable record of 33 years at sea without injury to crew and every voyage profitable.

Elsbeth II was on bare boat charter in Brazil at the time these pictures were taken. *Elsbeth III* was in Curacao, Netherlandfs Antilles, just back from having towed a disabled reefer ship with a cargo of perishable seafood from Cuba to Spain.

As *Rhea*, Smith Maritime's newest tug, was readied for sea trials, AB Patrick Bruno (left), a native of Dominique in the Caribbean, prepares to apply additional deck surfacing. Close to the family, he was born in the same hospital, same year, as Dom Smith, only son in the family and also a tugboat captain and McAllister Towing and Transportation's port captain in Baltimore.

Rhea has three 16-cylinder Cummins Diesels that produce 5,000HP. She has a bow thruster and six rudders. Her propellers are Kort-nozzled for protection and added thrust. She is just shy of 90 feet long. Her engine and propulsion specs are all built with the life of a sea-going, long-haul tug in mind—built for lengthy runs, heavy loads and rising seas.

New Orleans, Louisiana

E.N. Bisso & Son, Inc.

Just before ending its long southward journey to the Gulf of Mexico, the last 234 miles of America's mighty Mississippi River flow past four of the country's major seaports: Baton Rouge, located at the convergence of the Mississppi River and the Gulf Intercoastal Waterway, ranked 7th by total tons handled in 1999; Plaquemine, ranked 8th; New Orleans, ranked 4th in the same year; and the Port of South Louisiana, closest to the Gulf, which is at the top of the list of US ports in terms of tonnage handled.

These four seaports, all on Louisiana's Lower Mississippi River, make up the world's busiest port complex and accounted for 428 million tons of cargo in 1999—a third of the total of 1.4 billion tons handled by the 20 top ports in the country.

These statistics translate into more than 10,000 deep-draft vessel calls per year to this four-port region, plus countless numbers of barges which, in the Port of South Louisiana alone, totaled more than 50,000. All of this traffic means that an average of fifty inbound and out-bound vessels travel these waters each day with many, if not most, needing tugboat assistance.

Four marine towing companies—E. N. Bisso & Son, Inc., Bisso Towboat Company, Inc., Crescent Towing and Salvage Company, Inc., and River Parishes Company—handle most of this ship-assist work. The two Bisso companies are not related and competition among them is fierce. In 1995, when Walter K. Kristiansen joined E. N. Bisso as Chief Operating Officer, the firm's share of this huge ship-assist market stood at 18 percent. Now, seven years later, and with Kristiansen as president and CEO since 1999, it has almost doubled to 34 percent.

That kind of a shift does not happen by accident. A soft-spoken leader in the US towboat industry, Kristiansen's strength lies in his unflinching belief in his three major constituencies—his employees, his customers and his stockholders. His employees, 150 strong, are honed and treated like family with reciprocity an expectation, though he teaches and favors strong lines of demarcation between boat captains, often referred to as "co-presidents of the tugs," or between department heads and their subordinates. E. N. Bisso's customers are offered strong guarantees and promises such as on-time arrivals of the tugs, no "overtime" charge for any tug service, and no requirement for a minimum period of hourly work, which differentiate the company from its competitors. And Kristiansen firmly believes that his stockholders are entitled to a realistic return on their investment. Even in tough times, the company has remained profitable.

Robert Johnson, captain of the *Vera Bisso*, and Walter Kristiansen, president, E. N. Bisso & Son, Inc., in the *Vera Bisso*'s pilot house. With 360-degree, deck-to-overhead panoramic glass, visibility is always excellent.

As a marine towboat operator on the Mississippi River, E. N.Bisso, under Walter Kristiansen's leadership, has developed a tugboat-design philosophy that runs counter to the surge towards Z-drive tugs.

"We believe that the Mississippi, because of its strong currents and the large amount of flotsam that floats downstream—lumber, buoys that are torn from their location, metal debris, almost anything imaginable—presents a special challenge to tug design, especially to the propellers. Therefore, even our newest boat, the Vera Bisso, *has very large stainless steel conventional propellers, eleven 1/2 feet in diameter, housed in Kort nozzles. Each one weighs 12 tons and, we believe, is less vulnerable to the rigors of the river."*

At an "honest" horsepower rating of 3950HP, *Vera Bisso*'s two 16-cylinder EMD's generate a strong bollard pull rating* of 70 tons. Kristiansen maintains:

"A tugboat is just a piece of steel with an engine in it, pushing or pulling on a larger piece of steel with an engine in it. We strongly believe in having great equipment like this three-year-old vessel and great crews to run her. If you take a tug like the Vera Bisso *and place it in the hands of second-rate crews, you might as well have an outboard out there.*

"It took only a week of company meetings to come up with our input for the Vera Bisso's *design. We wanted a tug with great maneuverability that could remain perpendicular to a ship in the Mississippi's various river conditions. We were concerned that Z-drives would be more vulnerable to debris floating downstream so we ended up with two main steering rudders aft and two sets of flanking rudders, all of which can be turned independently. We call the* Vera Bisso *an 'enhanced twin-screw' tug.*

"We also call her the 'green boat' as we tried hard to look ahead into the future and anticipate new environmental regulations. Our tanks containing pollutants are built away from the outside of the tug. We tried to learn from tankers and our fuel tanks on the boat do not vent to the atmosphere. In addition, each fuel tank is separately alarmed and, if it does get overfilled, the excess goes into a line and into an overflow tank with a 1200-gallon capacity which is alarmed to go off at 25 gallons, leaving plenty of time for response."

*Towing power of a tug measured under prescribed conditions.

Vera Bisso moves swiftly on the Mississippi River. Two 16-cylinder EMD's produce 3950HP and a strong bollard pull rating of 70 tons.

This latest E. N. Bisso tug is built for harbor work, which is what most of their customers want. She meets ABS A1 Maltese Cross standards. With the addition of some deck machinery, some additional electronics and reallocation of tankage, *Vera Bisso* can be ready to go offshore within about two weeks.

One of her captains, Robert Johnson, joined the company right out of high school in 1974. Starting on the *Jackie B* as a deckhand, he then spent 20 years aboard the *Gladys B,* famous for her teak decks. Now he is assigned to the *Vera Bisso* on a seven-days-on, seven-days-off schedule and loves it.

"She is a very stable, good-handling, all-around comfortable boat. We use a special nine-inch Plasma™ line for making up to ships. All the deckhand has to do is get the heaving line aboard the vessel and I do the rest from the wheelhouse, feeding out the line over the winch as the vessel we are working needs it. Life for the deckhands has become so easy, they sometimes refer to themselves as only 'window washers' because of the 360-degree, deck-to-overhead panoramic glass in the pilot house. That's a lot of glass!"

They work hard on the upkeep of the vessel. A working tug now for three years, she looks like she's just been commissioned, right out of the shipyard. In addition to her environmental sensitivities, she also sports a unique set of safety features, a natural result in a safety-conscious company: the engine room contains three water-tight doors with an additional enclosed ladder to the deckhouse; seven feet of space between the deckhouse and the higher-than-normal 39-inch bulwarks that creates a broad and extremely safe deck area; deckhouse portholes two feet in diameter, allowing escape routes for even the heaviest crew members; even though the tug's bow is shaped, her bow fendering is flat, allowing for easy perpendicular positioning of tug to ship; and the wheelhouse is especially bright, with windows flanged inward for easy make-ups to ships, and heads-up displays of navigation aids and key systems monitors.

Walter Kristiansen believes in good crews afloat and ashore. He knows that he succeeds only when the shore managers, captains, crews, dispatchers and maintenance and administrative staff are equally successful. Everyone at E. N. Bisso works toward these goals. His VP of Operations, Bill Summers, has been aboard for a year. A graduate of the United States Merchant Marine Academy at Kings Point, NY, Bill holds a chief engineer's license. He worked

Vera Bisso leads E. N. Bisso & Son's tug fleet on the Mississippi River. She was built with two large conventional stainless steel propellers, rather than the Z-drive propulsion so often used now, because the company believes that the Mississippi River's strong currents and large amounts of river debris present a special challenge to propeller design.

in the offshore oil industry for more than 30 years, in and out of ports like Port Fourchon, LA, which he has seen explode in terms of the level of activity and OSV (offshore supply vessel) traffic there. His wide range of responsibilities at E. N. Bisso include the maintenance operations, crews, safety issues—literally everything except sales and even there he uses his offshore contacts to drum up business.

Ned Breedon, just four weeks with the company when we met and recently with NASA, has assumed the title of Coordinator of Quality Assurance, Training and Compliance. He brings a whole new area of expertise to a marine towing firm in which quality of service and safety issues are the highest priority.

With the four-port region on Louisiana's Lower Mississippi River covering an area of 234 miles, the E. N. Bisso fleet of tugs is spread out on various points of the river, eliminating, most of the time, the need to run tugs for long distances up or downstream. By and large, the Baton Rouge and Plaquemine jobs are handled by the boats there, while the New Orleans area jobs and work below the 100-mile marker are handled out of fleet headquarters in Metairie. Working out of their corporate offices, Walter Kristiansen stands at the helm of the entire operation.

"Marine towing, like any business, requires tight management if the bottom line is to come out right. Our operational leadership team deals with three levels of priorities when it comes to doing work on the fleet. The first priority, always, consists of safety and seaworthiness issues. At the second level, we will deal with questions of efficiency, i.e. a propeller has a few dings in it causing some excess vibrations. We correct that as soon as we can. Third, we will face what we call gingerbread or nice-to-have items such as a stack that needs painting. At that level it gets to be a little like elective surgery—we'll tackle it when the budget and time permit."

Whatever E. N.Bisso is doing on the Lower Mississippi, they must be doing it right. A unique team, they remain a major player on America's Old Man River—an important link in the economy of the country.

Vera Bisso is the company's "green boat," built with a deep respect for environmental issues. Tanks containing pollutants are built away from the outside of the tug. Fuel tanks do not vent into the atmosphere and are separately alarmed and built with overflow going straight to a 1200-gallon capacity overflow tank. Designed basically for harbor work, *Vera Bisso* can be adapted for offshore duty within a two-week time frame.

Known throughout the world as "Old Man River," the Mississippi River, 2,300 miles long, has its source in Minnesota at 1,475 feet above sea level. Through a large system of locks maintained by the US Army Corps of Engineers, the river is kept on course, dropping the entire elevation by the time it reaches the Gulf of Mexico in the state of Louisiana. It runs through or borders eight other US states—Wisconsin, Iowa, Illinois, Missouri, Kentucky, Tennessee, Arkansas and Louisiana.

At its beginning, its width is 20–30 feet; its widest point measures nearly a mile across, just south of its confluence with the Missouri River near Alton, Illinois.

Less than three feet deep at its headwaters, the Mississippi is deepest in New Orleans at 200 feet. It is deep-draft navigable from the Gulf of Mexico to Baton Rouge, Louisiana through a channel at least 45-feet deep. From there, up river to St. Paul, Minnesota, a channel of at least nine feet in depth is maintained, all by the US Army's Corps of Engineers.

The *L.J. Sullivan*, shown here pushing a tow of four bulk barges south on the river, is a typical Mississippi River towboat. Capable of pushing many more barges at a time, these vessels are the backbone of the river's huge commercial impact.

Sixty percent of all grain exported from the United States is shipped via the Mississippi River and through the ports of New Orleans and South Louisiana. In terms of tonnage, the largest port in the world is located in LaPlace, Louisiana. Between the two of them, the Port of New Orleans and the Port of South Louisiana shipped more than 243 million tons of goods in 1999. Shipping on the lower end of the Mississippi River is focused on petroleum, iron and steel, grain, rubber, paper and wood, coffee, coal, chemicals and edible oils. (data courtesy of the National Park Service and the St. Paul, Minnesota Port Authority's video: "Mississippi: The Working River".)

Port Fourchon, Louisiana

Captain Philip Ledet and Captain Chris Duet

Captain Philip Ledet

Captain Chris Duet

Parish LaFourche ("the Fork" in French) is located along the Gulf coast in southeastern Louisiana, about 100 miles to the southwest of New Orleans. In the heart of Cajun country, the "po'boy" sandwiches are great and so are the gumbos and seafood. Here, you can certainly get by without being able to speak French, but it definately helps if you do.

Bayou LaFourche is the parish's main water artery, flowing in a slightly southeasterly direction for some 140 miles from its beginning near Donaldsonville on the Mississippi River.

The area is extremely flat and very pretty, laced with inland waterways. It is home to three major industries that compete for space and workers: agriculture, mostly in the raising of sugar cane; shrimping; and the offshore oil and gas industry, with more than 350 drilling platforms in the Gulf of Mexico, all of which are serviced by local businesses through local ports.

Captain Philip Ledet, a tall, handsome, wiry man, is the operations manager of the Dolphin Towing Company, located in Galliano, Louisiana, right on the banks of Bayou LaFourche, 25 miles north of Port Fourchon at the Bayou's mouth. He was born and raised here in the heart of Cajun country, graduating from South LaFourche High School in 1968.

Dolphin's fleet consists of four vessels, all working out of Port Fourchon. Ledet is currently buying a fifth boat, while a sixth is already on the drawing boards.

"We don't yet know where it will be built—but it will be around here somewhere. There are shipyards in Lockport, Houma, Larose, and even New Orleans isn't that far away.

"Our work is strictly offshore; our smallest tug is 110 feet long and has diesels that provide 9,000HP. The next largest boat measures 135 feet with 14,500HP and the other two are each 150 feet in length, one with 13,500HP and one with 16,500HP. Most of our work is moving drilling rigs, either from one location to another or from port to offshore or offshore back to port. We also do a lot of construction work, moving derrick and pipe-laying barges. Those barges are anchored with what we call 'eight-point anchor spreads' to keep them as stable as possible in the Gulf's waters.

"Typical crew numbers for us are five on the smaller vessels and seven on the larger. Of course, it all depends on the work involved: if we are working with a pipe-laying barge that has to be moved 24 hours a day—and that means hauling and re-setting those eight anchors every time—a five-man crew can easily grow to nine. A typical duty hitch is 28 days on and 14 days off."

Philip Ledet holds a 1600-ton master's license as well as one as an unlimited chief engineer.

Tugs *Jennifer* and *Tampa Bay* at the ready on Louisiana's Bayou LaFourche.

Like many mariners, he comes from a family of seamen, though most of them were commercial fishermen, working shrimp, oysters and finfish until the fishing industry began its decline. Now most of the seamen in his family work on the tugs or the supply vessels that run back and forth to the rigs in the Gulf.

Like most local seamen, Captain Ledet started out as a deckhand on his father's boat while still in high school and worked his way up through the ranks.

"Much of the cargo coming down Bayou LaFourche, right by the building here, is destined for the offshore rigs. Usually the barges end up in Port Fourchon and the load is then transferred to an offshore supply vessel (OSV). We also have 'Anchor-Handling Tug Supply Boats' which have the capability of doing supply runs, anchor handling and towing—very versatile vessels.

"There are more than 350 drilling platforms in the Gulf of Mexico, the farthest being about 150 miles offshore. The rigs that are closer to the shoreline are often what we call 'jack-up rigs' or 'shallow-water rigs'. Once the legs are set in the seabed, they can raise the rig platform right out of the water. Next we have a 'semi rig,' which refers to the fact that it is semi-submergible. That rig floats and, like the 'jack-ups', is quite easily moved from one location to another and then held in place by that same eight-point anchor spread. The third kind of rig is a 'platform rig' which sits on an existing structure. Those are more permanently sited although they can be moved by disassembling them and placing them on a supply boat to be moved to another structure.

"Working the Gulf waters, running between the rigs that produce the oil and gas can be terrific on the calmer days, not so much fun as the weather gets bad. When you're towing heavy loads like barges or rigs, there is always the danger that your tow will sink and pull the towboat down with it. That has certainly happened. If you come into a turn too fast and the tension on the tow cable isn't what it needs to be, your tow can pass you and capsize your boat. That's happened too. One thing you must learn early on as a seaman is that the sea is not very forgiving. You have to play its conditions fairly and with deep respect."

The rhythm of business in the work Dolphin Towing does differs from more typical tugboat operations. Although jobs come less frequently, they usually pay more. The firm does well when the boats are working 50% of the time, which makes for happier crews and more time for maintenance. The movement of rigs is always the result of a bidding process. Philip adds:

"We get our fair share of the business and sometimes we guess right, sometimes wrong. But in the long run, we're doing all right. There are cycles, of course, like in any business— hurricane season from July through October is one determinant. The health of the oil and gas industry is another and, at year's end, budgets are all used and our business slows. We expect that. But each day brings its own challenges and it surely is never boring!

Picture-perfect tug *Vivian* is reflected on the calm waters of Bayou LaFourche, main waterway to Port Fourchon at the Bayou's mouth. The port is a major gateway to the Gulf of Mexico's oil and gas industry. There are more than 350 drilling platforms in the Gulf.

"Of course our competitors are building larger vessels now as well. As the rigs move farther and farther out to sea, the tugs all of us build need to be bigger with more horse-power and have to be fitted for longer range missions. That can mean larger fuel and water tanks, bigger crew quarters and so on. It's a constantly evolving business. As an example, years ago the largest OSV was 200 feet long with a beam of 38 feet—now the bigger supply boats are at least 50 feet longer and their beam is more like 55 feet. During that same time period the range of the vessels has tripled."

A few miles farther south is Port Fourchon. Captain Chris Duet is on board Dolphin Towing Company's brand-new vessel, *DuMar III*. She is a "towing and anchor-handling tug" and is only three months old. One hundred and fifty feet long with a 50-foot beam, she generates 16,500HP from her two turbo engines and is state-of-the-art from bow to stern. She carries 300,000 gallons of fuel, 6,000 gallons of engine lubricant and 20,000 gallons of potable water. There are seven bunk rooms with berths for 18 crew members.

Port Fourchon has grown from a rather small, insignificant port in the mid 1970s to a hub of offshore support services activity in the central Gulf of Mexico today. Since oil and gas support services are its niche market, the level of activity in the port reflects the cycles in that market-place. In the 1980s, oil and gas experienced dramatic lows. Companies, forced to downsize, recognized that they must consolidate their numerous facilities throughout coastal Louisiana into one or two logistically advantageous locations. Port Fourchon benefited from that process and experienced huge growth during those times. It is now seeking to move beyond the one industry it knows best to examine the possibilities of becoming a major trading port with Latin American countries to its south.

Captain Chris Duet first went to sea 32 years ago, when he was 15 years old, aboard a 300HP single-screw tug his uncle owned.

"The electric system had 32 volts and you took a shower with a garden hose! I was an undocumented captain by the time I was 19."

Born and raised in Louisiana, Captain Duet has spent the last dozen years in tugboats on the east coast. Now, after the raising of his six children and counting eight grandkids—his own parents having died early in 2001—he heeded Philip Ledet's call to come back to the bayou and captain the newest Dolphin boat, the *DuMar III*.

"I've done different things in my life such as working for Dow Chemical, Schlumberger, Haliburton Services, usually on offshore supply vessels. But mostly I've been on tugboats and there have been quite a few hair-raising experiences such as when we were towing containers from Jacksonville, Florida to Port Elizabeth, New Jersey or from Port Everglades, Florida to San Juan, Puerto Rico. Those trips around Cape Hatteras, especially in the winter, are something to remember forever. I'm getting to the point now where my sense of adventure isn't quite what it used to be. The bumps and bruises seem to take longer to heal now and I'm not so much of a cowboy anymore.

"Right after taking delivery of DuMar III *last October, we were fortunate in landing three fairly big jobs in a row. So we've been to sea on this vessel quite a bit over recent months and we're getting to know her pretty well. Moving through the oil fields has its own set of problems, of course. The targets are mostly stationary, not moving as they are on an Inter-state. Much of the work is done at night, often in tough weather conditions. It's the best work for the boats though, because, in moving the rigs, there is no hull-to-hull contact with other vessels as there is in pushing barges or in the docking and undocking of larger vessels.*

"When starting out, there is always a tug on the bow or forward center-point of the rig and two other boats on the port and starboard legs. Once we get off location, the two outside boats come up front and all three of us then pull together from the bow position. About a mile or two before getting to the new location, the two outside tugs drop back and make fast to the stern legs of the rig and that gives us a good balance then as to for-ward, backward and sideways motion to nudge the rig into its new position. The length of the tows can vary greatly. The first job we did with DuMar III *was 200 miles long. But they*

can be as short as a mile or two. When you get a long-range job, and especially if it runs smoothly, without incident, that's a good economic shot in the arm for the company and, in the long run, for all of us. Right now, at the end of the year, it's a little slow—but we expect that. By the end of February business usually picks up dramatically. Of course we are quite weather-dependent as well, especially with the jack-up rigs. They tend to be more vulnerable to winter weather. As the legs get set and the platform raises up, swells easily get in underneath and can fairly easily wreak havoc with the jack-up gear mechanisms. So they are used less during the rougher winter weather months. Our busiest time runs from early April through October though, starting in July, we keep a sharp lookout for hurricanes. Do we come back to port when a hurricane is forecast? No, not usually—that's for the other guys. We're supposed to be doing the rescuing out there, if needed.

"I put all the equipment on the bridge on board the DuMar III myself. When I first saw her, this bridge was like an empty loft. The only thing we had was the 96 windows. I came on board in late May and we took her out of the shipyard towards the end of October, so we spent five months outfitting her. I've taken over a few new boats before, which usually requires only a fresh coat of paint and you're off. But this time, Philip Ledet said, 'OK, this is going to be your boat, you finish her the way you want her.' So I spent a lot of time looking at blueprints, then started cutting out cardboard footprints of the different things we were going to install. I was like a kid in a toy store because I love electronics, unlike some of the older captains who will settle for a compass and maybe GPS (Global Positioning System)."

Rightfully so, Captain Duet is proud of his accomplishment. DuMar III's bridge is beautiful as well as functional, with the roomiest wheelhouse I have ever seen on a tugboat. He praises the company and Captain Ledet for being so supportive in building the vessel in a manner that allowed him—the incoming captain—the best operational handling. Looking out the rear windows of the bridge towards the stern of the vessel, over the wide aft deck full of the equipment that makes towing as well as anchor-handling easier and safer, I am struck with the energy DuMar III displays. Most tugboats appear powerful as they steam towards you, their stubby bows breaking seas as they approach. This towing and anchor-handling vessel displays its strength aft as well as forward. She reminds me of a quarterhorse on a farm—strong, agile and speedy—with few tasks she couldn't handle. What a boat!

DuMar III in Port Fourchon, Louisiana. Dolphin Towing Company's new anchor handling tug, she is the pride of the fleet. With a length of 150 and a beam of 50 feet, DuMar III is rated at 16,500HP. She can carry 300,000 gallons of fuel, 6,000 gallons of engine lubricant and 20,000+ gallons of potable water.

Chicago, Illinois

Captain Jeff Henderson

The Calumet River spills into Lake Michigan on Chicago's South Shore, just west of the Indiana line. Great Lakes Towing Company, better known as "GLT" or "The Towing Company," has its Chicago docks here along with five of its fleet of 50 vessels. Formed in 1898, GLT is headquartered in Cleveland and its centralized dispatch operation works out of that port. Those needing ship-assistance on the Great Lakes or in any of the region's 11 major ports, call GLT's Cleveland dispatch office. GLT does almost all of the ship-assist work on the Great Lakes with just eight to ten of its fleet of tugs assigned to offshore or "outside" towing.

Ship-assist business on the Great Lakes is not as good as it used to be. There are fewer ore ships bringing product mined in Minnesota and Wisconsin down to the steel mills in Cleveland, Chicago, Toledo and Detroit. In many cases, newer vessels are now equipped with bow and stern thrusters and are therefore less likely to need tug assistance. Though most of the tugs in the GLT fleet are more than 70 years old—all single-screw boats that were converted from steam to diesel in the 1950s and 60s, with horsepower ranging from 800 to 1200HP—they are strong, scrappy boats that are perfect for the jobs they are required to do. GLT has the largest fleet of tugs in the world in that horsepower range.

At the time of our interview, in May 2002, the majority of incoming Great Lakes cargo consisted of imported steel, coming from overseas on ocean-going vessels called "salties" by the local mariners. With US trade policy raising tariffs on these products, that may soon change. The same ships that bring steel in hope to pick up a cargo of grain for their outbound voyage. The steel is usually unloaded in Cleveland or Chicago and the grain is most often picked up for export in Superior or Duluth.

GLT tugboats are crewed by a captain, an engineer, and a deckhand with all positions unionized. Captains and engineers belong to the Masters, Mates and Pilots union while the deckhands are represented by the SIU. The lack of work has hit the marine industry on the Great Lakes hard, with GLT doing about a third less in the last navigational season than the one before. Navigational seasons are defined from when the ice leaves the lakes in the spring of the year (most often early April) to when they freeze over again, usually around the end of December. The company measures its production by the number of lines being made up to a

The Great Lakes Towing Company, headquartered in Cleveland, Ohio, does the majority of the ship-assist work on the Great Lakes. The company dates back to 1898. Its fleet of 50 tugs with horsepower ratings averaging 800-1200HP is the largest in the world at that level.

The tug *South Carolina* heads out to a barge job on Chicago's Calumet River. Because many of the bridges in the Great Lakes' eleven major ports have low clearances, GLT tugs are built close to the water.

ship or barge, with GLT staffed to handle approximately 5,000 lines in a given navigational period. Most tugs are laid up during the off-season, though some ports may keep one or two boats "hot" so they can be used for icebreaking by keeping an onboard oil-fired low pressure steam boiler running.

Captain Jeff Henderson has been with the company for two and a half years and is GLT's port representative for their Chicago operation. Together with his yard manager, Harold Rodriguez, he is responsible for keeping the GLT tugs in Chicago operable, ready to respond to any request by a Cleveland dispatcher. He has been in the marine industry all his life, growing up in Florida, working professionally in the oil fields off the southern coasts of Texas and Louisiana, where he captained a crew boat. Jeff has also done substantial work as a marine surveyor.

Beaumont/Port Arthur, Texas

Moran Towing of Texas

Stephen M. Kelly is the Vice President and General Manager of Moran Towing of Texas, Inc., headquartered in Nederland, Texas. He has been with Moran for more than 20 years and in his present job for about 12 months. Nederland is near the Sabine-Neches Ship Channel, which brings commercial marine traffic to the Port of Beaumont from the Gulf of Mexico. Formed by the Sabine and Neches Rivers, the federally maintained channel runs 42 miles upstream from the Gulf, with a minimum width of 400 and minimum depth of 40 feet.

A series of jetties, canals, rivers and turning basins comprise the waterway. The Port of Sabine Pass is at the mouth of the channel with jetties extending three miles into the Gulf. Twenty-four miles north is Port Arthur, where the Sabine-Neches Waterway then splits, with Beaumont 19 miles up the Neches River to the west and the Port of Orange 15 miles above the junction to the east and accessible via the Sabine River and the Intracoastal Canal.

Four Moran tugs—the *Cape Ann, Helen Moran, Mary Moran* and *Michael Turecamo*—comprise Steve Kelly's fleet. Their competitor, Sea Bulk, also has four boats and together, the eight tugs service the district.

Captain John H. Toups and his protégé, Quarter-master Tommy Placette, plan strategy for the next ship-assist job. Moran Towing of Texas' four tugs, including *Michael Turecamo*, are based on the Sabine-Neches Waterway.

"This four-port area is a great place to view a variety of marine activity. On the waterfront where two of our tugs are docked, you will see inland push boats moving anywhere from one to six barges with very large ocean going freighters and tankers passing by them. That's one of the problems here, with both ends of the seagoing commerce spectrum active on any given day. There are the very large ships and, because of the connections to the inland waterways, we have a great deal of inland work as well. In addition, down in the Sabine Lake area, there is a sizeable mothball fleet. No gunships but quite a few older freighters, like the Liberty ships of World War II fame, and tankers, that can be readied fairly quickly again if needed to carry freight or petroleum products in time of war. An older aircraft carrier, the USS Oriskiny, is also anchored there now. She is the carrier from which Senator John McCain flew when he was shot down during the war in Vietnam.

"I mention the anchorage because it adds to the creation of very busy waterways in this four-port Sabine-Neches district, which has become the second-largest port facility in Texas, right behind that of Galveston-Houston-Texas City. That means being extremely careful as ships and tows move through.

"Though tides are not a concern here because they are so minimal, hours of daylight are very important. Many of the ships coming into the Port of Beaumont are so large that they have 'restrictions' on them, which often means that shipping traffic can go only one way. Since it takes eight hours, on average, to bring a large ship up the channel, traffic on any given day probably can move only one way in the winter months when there are just about eight hours of daylight. Summer daylight hours being much longer, we can often time a series of inbound and outbound activities on the same day. An example of how critical these timings can be: if a ship arrives offshore at 1100 on a given winter day, it cannot begin to proceed up the channel. So it anchors offshore. If it so happens that outbound traffic has been scheduled for the following day, it cannot enter port until the third day. Of course, the clock is always ticking for the owners of the vessels so this is something they do not like to see.

"Back in the early 80's, when I first came here, we were still operating single-screw tugs. We had the E. M. Black, built in 1936, the original Stella Moran, built in 1910, and two other vessels, the Helen Moran and the Mary Moran. Today, all our tugs have twin-screws and range in horsepower from 3000 to 4700, which are pretty much the minimums now needed to move the ever-larger ships being built."

More than 80% of the cargo moved in the Sabine-Neches port district is oil or petroleum derivatives like coke, which is used in the blackening of tire walls and sometimes used for fuel in place of coal. Much of the remaining traffic consists of whatever is shipped from the public docks, like military supplies, and bulk goods such as grain.

When we finished our interview, Steve Kelly directed me to the waterfront in search of Captain John H. Toups of the *Mary Moran*. She was moored in Port Arthur at the vessel repair shipyard, right on the banks of the Sabine-Neches Waterway, just as I had been told. Toups and his quartermaster, a young captain-in-training named Tommy Placette, came ashore and we spoke beside the tug *Michael Turecamo*, a Moran boat that used to belong to Turecamo before Moran bought that company. *Mary Moran* was rafted to her starboard side and there were shrimpers fore and aft. As Kelly had said, it was a busy waterway. Captain John Toups personified the tugboat professional Steve Kelly had earlier described. Toups grew up on the southernmost tip of Texas, in Sabine Pass, just across the water from Louisiana's Sabine National Wildlife Refuge. His earliest recollections include ocean-going ships moving up and down the waterway, literally past his house. Attending high school to tenth grade, he was illiterate until he was 27 years old. His speech and looks reflected the maritime life he had led.

Toups joined the tugboat community in 1957 as a deckhand on the tug *John B.* One year later, he came aboard another single-screw boat, the *E. M. Black*, which was owned at that time by the Picton Towing Company, a predecessor business to Moran Towing of Texas. Most of the time was spent working construction sites, moving crane barges and occasionally dumping dredged material out to sea. One fateful day, a new captain named Eckelson came aboard. Both he and his wife, who worked with special-needs children, seemed especially interested

The tug *Cape Ann*, of Moran Towing of Texas, leaves her dock to meet an inbound Greek bulk freighter headed for the Port of Beaumont. A twin-screw, 4800HP tug, she is the most powerful of the four Moran tugs in Texas.

in helping children with their schooling, showing particular interest in teaching them to read. After trying to start a discussion with John about the Dr. Seuss books, Eckelson realized that Toups could not read. He immediately began a tutoring regimen, taking his own time off to work with the deckhand one day a week. Within twelve weeks, John was reading well enough to take some courses at a maritime school. He remains grateful to his mentor to this day.

Captain Toups has now been working with Moran for 42 years. His first licenses included a 200-ton inland operator's document which allowed him to work on western rivers. He earned his first captain's license 30 years ago and now holds a 1600-ton master's paper. He calls his tug, the *Mary Moran*, "the best boat afloat" and lauds his crew, an engineer, a quartermaster and a deckhand, as well. The quartermaster, Tommy Placette, is the son of Moran of Texas' dispatcher, a tugboater for five years. He is also like a son to John Toups since his own family consists of a wife and five daughters. Toups knows the value of a parent, having lost his own dad in a pilot boat accident when he was only five. Young and scrappy, Placette is the beneficiary of all that history, with the support of two "dads." His quartermaster license allows him to drive the tug when the captain asks him to do so. Like most who come into the tugboat fraternity, Placette started as an ordinary seaman, then took Coast Guard courses and worked his way up to able bodied seaman. He explains:

"Once you are an AB, you can start working towards the various licenses, beginning with the 200-ton paper, which I have earned. Most people in the tugboat industry want to reach the 1600-ton license and that's what I'm working towards. That's really plenty for tugboats, which rarely reach weight designations more than several hundred tons. There are also differences in licenses—like inland and near-coastal, for example. Mine is the latter, which is better because it enables me to work offshore. We assist anywhere from one to five vessels a day. Every so often we'll have some down time, but that is almost always short-lived. Then we have periods where we just keep going around the clock and you find yourself really dragging at the end.

"I was sort of born into the business, you know, with my dad being a Moran dispatcher. They call him 'Chunky' and I've always known him by that name too. When I was in first

The *S/R Charleston* gets turned 180 degrees in the Port of Beaumont's turning basin. Riding fairly high out of the water, she will pick up petroleum product at a refinery down river.

grade and they asked us to write down our parents' names, that's what I wrote. Everyone laughed and I cried because I didn't know what I had done wrong. When I came home from school there would often be a captain there, talking with my dad—and I'd hear the radio or phone conversations, all the arguing about shifts and all, and I'd swear to myself that I wouldn't do that in a million years. But I also heard that there was good money in it and there is and here I am. Out of high school, I went into auto body and fender repair work and did that for two and a half years. When I wanted to buy a new truck, I realized I wasn't going to get far on six bucks an hour. My dad had been after me for years to get on the boats and finally convinced me and saw to it that I could be working for several different captains, Captain Toups included. They don't come any better.

"It took me a while to get into it, especially the taking-orders bit and that everything had to be done so quickly, 'chop-chop', no hesitations. I had come out of a high school where everyone stood up for himself, fought for himself. Suddenly I found myself needing to take orders from others, no back talk tolerated. It was like being in the service and I was not used to that—but I sure am now. I was fired once for 28 days for not following orders and I went through a lot of ridicule, people dragging my name through the mud, but I stuck it out. The only one who stood by me was Captain Toups."

Before leaving the vessel repair area to head upstream to the Port of Beaumont, I took a last look at the two hefty Moran tugs secured to the shipping channel's western shore. They looked poised and tough, ready for their next assignments.

In Beaumont, John Maxey, captain of the tug *Helen Moran*, came off his boat to meet me. A 3500HP tug and 101 feet in length, she and her Moran partner *Cape Ann*, do a great deal of

The Port of Beaumont/ Port Arthur is always among the top ten US ports measured in tonnage handled. That is because very large, 100,000+ ton, tankers call here often. They usually have to offload some of their cargo offshore to reduce their draft, enabling them to transit the Sabine-Neches Waterway. The *S/R Charleston* is being escorted by a Sea Bulk tug.

Cape Ann prepares for action late on an especially beautiful Texas afternoon. Moran Towing of Texas' four tugs handle about 60 vessels each month. The company's main competitor works a similar amount of vessel traffic.

the ship-assist work in Beaumont. Maxey is a mild-looking man and, if I had to guess his occupation, I'd think of agricultural machinery, not tugboats. But tugboats it has been—the last 25 years with Moran.

"The biggest part of our business here is petroleum-related even though there are no oil docks. The port of Beaumont/Port Arthur is a busy US seaport, always rated in the top ten per tonnage handled. That is mostly because we get huge 100,000 and up ton tankers, some of which need to have a portion of their cargo unloaded by lighters before they can make it in to port. Because the water depth in the Gulf is fairly shallow—15 miles out it is still only 40 feet—some of these bigger tankers anchor 100 miles out to sea to begin this offloading. The ship just ahead of us here is loading grain and in about an hour, we have a bulk carrier coming in to load assorted cargo at one of the city docks. Tonight we will be moving the grain ship to an anchorage where she will take on fuel from bunker barges. We probably handle about 60 ships a month, inbound and then outbound, and our competition handles a similar number."

Just as the setting sun begins to splay its golden rays across the river, two large inbound ships appear, a Greek bulk carrier and the tanker S/R Charleston. The bulker proceeds straight in to its dock, while the tanker is turned 180 degrees to face down-channel for its final few miles of return to the Port Arthur refinery. It had been a day full of tugboat history and stories eagerly shared by the crews. Thanks to them, I had learned much about South Texas ports and the maritime business there.

San Diego, California

Edison Chouest Offshore

As American commercial ports go, San Diego, California, is not especially big, yet, it is home to one of the largest naval installations in the world, Naval Station San Diego. More than 70 naval vessels of all types are based here and naval aviation was born across the bay at Coronado Naval Air Station.

Three major tugboat companies—Edison Chouest Offshore, Crowley Marine Services, and Foss Maritime—service the San Diego waterfront, assisting naval as well as non-military vessels. Through the good work of Paul Castle, Operations Manager for Chouest's San Diego activities, who made it possible for me to get through the naval station's tight security, I was able to meet five of Chouest's captains, all skippers of their state-of-the-art tractor tugs. Robert Fletcher commands *C-Tractor Eight*; Kevin Caldwell, *C-Tractor Seven*; Steven Freitas, *C-Tractor Nine*; Steven Wareham, *C-Tractor Eleven*; and John LoCoco, *C-Tractor Fourteen*.

They are as skilled and dedicated a bunch of mariners as you are likely to find anywhere, and they know the waters of San Diego like the backs of their hands. At the time of the interviews, Chouest boats were under contract for a large percentage of the naval activity in the area, which kept the tugs off the dock, earning their keep, around the clock on many days.

Delving into the career backgrounds and sea experiences of the five skippers, this is what they had to say. Steven Freitas begins:

"I started out on tuna boats, which were once very big around here. I next went to work on offshore supply vessels doing supply and anchor-handling work for the oil rigs up in the Santa Barbara Channel. In 1989 my company received a contract for work back here

C-Tractor Eight, one of Edison Chouest Offshore's powerful San Diego tug fleet. The company is currently under contract to supply Naval Station San Diego's ship-assist needs. The top deck fender "wings" on Edison Chouest's C-Tractor tugs are designed specifically for use up against Navy ships whose hulls are often extremely concave. The photo on page 13 is an especially good example of this unique design application.

in San Diego and that is when I first joined the tugboat industry. More than a dozen years later, I'm still here!"

Steven Wareham adds:

"When I was a kid I went to sea on fishing boats out of Newport Beach, California, and quickly fell in love with the ocean. Long-range sport fishing came next, mostly between Los Angeles and San Diego. That took us out on multi-day trips for bigger game fish. I had always loved tugboats and what they do, especially the harbor work that is so much less-demanding than being offshore. One day I met Paul Castle here at Chouest and he brought me on board, starting as a deckhand. An early job was bringing one of the boats around from Louisiana, where she was built, through the Panama Canal and north to San Diego, a 29-day voyage.

"In addition to the deckhand skills I learned after joining Chouest, I was also able to get some experience in the engine room. Shortly after my 21st birthday, I obtained a Coast Guard captain's license and about five years ago, I was one of the first three captains promoted up through the ranks by our company."

John LoCoco reflects:

"In the late 1950's, my family had its own small albacore fishing boat right here in San Diego. So I was born to the water and have always enjoyed it. I remember fishing off-shore with my grandfather when I was small and later, as I grew up, I began tuna fishing commercially and did that for almost ten years.

"But in 1984, electronics, another passion of mine, lured me ashore and I worked in that business for nine years. Edison Chouest brought me back to the ocean, thankfully, in the early nineties. Like most of the guys, I started as a deckhand."

Robert Fletcher tells his story:

"My dad was a dentist, right here in San Diego, and from the time I was five years old he would take me out on his boats to fish. So I grew up loving the ocean and later, during summer breaks from high school, I started crewing on larger sports fishing vessels. Then, when I was 17, I started fishing commercially on tuna boats called "lift pole boats" and I have worked on them as far away as Australia. My west coast experiences have ranged

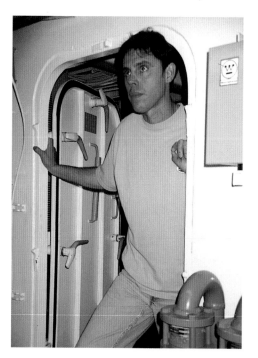

from Alaska all the way south to Panama, fishing for albacore and tuna. I did that for 15 years and then, like Steve Freitas, started working out of Santa Barbara on crew boats, running supplies and crews out to the oil rigs in the Channel.

"Then, as family responsibilities grew—we had two kids by then—I looked for work closer to home here in San Diego and began working on ferry boats and excursion vessels. That led to part-time work on tugs and, eventually, to Paul here at Edison Chouest where, like most of us, I began as a deckhand. Several months later I acquired some engine-room experience and soon had a 200-ton master's license, which made me more valuable to the company.

Kevin Caldwell joins in:

"I started working on fishing boats in Mexico Beach, Florida, when I was about 13. After a while I graduated to purse

Engineer Juan
Barandiaran

seine fishing. That's drawing a large net around a school of fish and closing it at the bottom, preventing their escape. It's a tactic often used for tuna but we were seeking bait fish at the time. By 1979 I had a chance to work in the Merchant Marine with a high school friend of mine and his father. We started in the Gulf of Mexico but were soon making overseas trips on a wide variety of jobs: pulling oil rigs, hauling anchors, pulling derrick barges to places in Africa, Peru, Jamaica, Egypt, Holland—lots of long tows!

"By 1985 I was in San Diego, working for another tugboat company. Soon Paul Castle recruited me as a deckhand and, like many of my mates here, I worked on deck and in the engine room until I was able to get a captain's license. It is the best job I have ever had!"

At this point, all five tractor tug masters joined in with effusive praise for their company, for its consistent commitment to give them the best there is in equipment and for the sense of family and camaraderie (their words) they experience here. I came away with the feeling that these men, their workplace and their company were unique. After the five captains had shared their career stories, I asked Paul Castle, Edison Chouest's Operations Manager, to add his own:

"My path to Edison Chouest and the civilian tugboat industry began in the Navy, where I spent 24 years both in the enlisted ranks and as a commissioned officer. Towards the end of my years in the military, I helped write a contract for the Navy's use of civilian tugs instead of the YTB's (the Navy's designation for its own tugboats). I was at King's Bay, Georgia, at the time and it was the second such contract written, San Diego having been the first. The transition from Navy to civilian tugs took about three years and Edison Chouest won that contract, which they still have. About three years later I retired from the Navy and joined Edison Chouest, working first for six months on their seismic vessel out of Galveston, Texas. Then I moved between San Diego and King's Bay twice before settling in here on the west coast in 1994 to supervise and administer our San Diego contract with the Navy and I've been here ever since."

Edison Chouest in San Diego works strictly on their Navy contract and handles other vessels only in emergencies. In incidents where non-Navy ships have lost power or steering or have experienced on-board fires, the nearest vessel comes to assist in the oldest of maritime traditions. It was great getting to know these guys who, aboard their C-Tractor Chouest tugs, keep America's Navy moving in one of its busiest installations.

Pictured above: most of Edison Chouest Offshore's San Diego based tug captains and their Operations Manager. Left to right, captains all: Stephen Wareham, *C-Tractor Eleven*; Kevin Caldwell, *C-Tractor Seven*; Bob Fletcher, *C- Tractor Eight*; Steven Freitas, *C-Tractor Nine*; John LoCoco, *C-Tractor Fourteen*; Paul Castle, Edison Chouest Offshore San Diego Operations Manager.

Captain Mark D. Jennings and Tom Summers, Engineer

Captain Mark Jennings

Engineer Tom Summers

Captain Mark D. Jennings is the skipper of the Foss Maritime tug *Pacific Queen*. Along with three other tugboats—*Pacific Knight, Pacific King* and *Pacific Viking*—they comprise the Foss fleet in San Diego harbor and handle much of the commercial ship traffic there.

"Though a conventional, twin-screw 2,000HP vessel, Pacific Queen *has a few bells and whistles that strengthen her pushing or towing capabilities and add to her maneuverability. Kort nozzles help direct the water flow through the vessel's propellers rather than allowing it to dissipate over their outer edges. Flanking rudders are rudders that are only used when you are moving astern. They actually sit in front of the screws. Since the regular rudders don't do you much good when moving astern, the flanking rudders take over, helping you direct all your wash on an astern bell. They are especially useful on river tows and were first developed for that kind of application."*

Captain Jennings is a San Diego native who has been in tugboating for 15 years. A 1983 graduate of the California Maritime Academy, he joined Scripps Oceanographic Institute and sailed all over the world on one of their research vessels. Before that, while still a cadet at the Academy, he came to San Diego on an internship at Foss' predecessor there, Pacific Towboat, known in the harbor as PACTOW.

"The work with the oceanographic institute was very interesting. I was on the Marathon Expedition, *doing a great deal of current metering work in the deep South Atlantic. But we also did a lot of topography studies, mostly for the US Navy, on the ocean beds. At the time we had something called the 'sea beam' system which allowed us to do more accurate mapping than was previously possible.*

"We would spend thirty days at a time in what is called the 'inter-tropical conversion zone' where the waters are extremely rough. To sleep, you would wedge yourself between life jackets on your bunk. They would form a cup of sorts and you would try to keep your body in it. You learn to sleep under those conditions but it's not much fun. The site was near what is known as the 'roaring forties' and we would do a lawn mower grid sweep of that part of the ocean to which we were assigned."

Like many mariners before him, Jennings realized that sailing the faraway oceans was lots of fun as a young man, but was not very compatible to a more normal family life. So, in 1987, he came back to San Diego full time.

"When I first went to work for PACTOW, I took a job few others seemed to want, towing a large oil barge up and down the west coast. Between offshore tows, I would work part time in the harbor, always as an engineer because my Academy degree was in engineering.

"One of the great things about running the tugs is that you never know what the next job will be. We do some Navy work, ship assist and offshore towing. We tow targets— those orange things you see tied up back there—a mile and a half behind the tug and we keep our fingers crossed that the gunners remain 'on target'. Since American naval vessels now board foreign shipping in different parts of the world, we do training with the crews here, having them board our tug as though we were a foreign ship.

"We tow barges up and down the coast and, in past years when the tuna fleet was healthier, we usually had a couple of tuna boat rescues a year. We tow barracks barges for the Navy—those are floating condominium sites that house the ship's crews when vessels undergo major repairs or overhauls. One of those is tied up on the port side of the carrier USS Nimitz back there in the carrier basin right now. Towing exercises are also part of our work, where Navy ships will use us as a vessel in distress and practice coming up against us to prepare to tow.

Pacific Queen engineer, Tom Summers was raised in Washington State and joined the Navy right out of high school, sailing on deck as a bosun's mate. After Vietnam and his discharge, he started crewing on sailboats, and one day found himself in Panama.

"After a while, I started getting hungry and needed a job. There was a large tuna fleet working out of Panama at the time, so I joined them as a seaman and began making the transition from the deck to the engine room by standing engine room watches. Before I knew it, 11 years had gone by and I was 33 with a lot of sea time in the engine room which qualified me for a US Coast Guard Assistant Engineer's license.

"Like so many things in life, after a while it got old. There was too much sea time—a couple of times I made 100-day trips back to back and, if it was a bad voyage, you could come back owing the boat money. So my next marine experience was working on off-shore oil rigs, mostly in the Gulf of Mexico, off Texas and Louisiana. Soon I was on anchor-handling tugs and that is where I first learned the towing business on large three-inch gear.

"Suddenly it seemed that a lot of my Navy experience was being put to use again. Many mariners feel that tugboats are the epitome of basic seamanship. And that is what we've been doing this morning. To me, it is very rewarding work with a good mix of thinking and critical activity. There was a time, after I was with Foss for a while, when I was laid off—there just wasn't enough work—and that afforded me an opportunity to do a wide variety of things: sailing, boat deliveries, working on two Americas Cups campaigns, to name a few. Five years ago I was recalled full time and I've been here since. I always love coming to work in the morning!"

A Military Sealift Command RoRo supply ship, used herre to train Naval Reservists up and down the west coast, is escorted through San Diego harbor by two Foss Maritime tugs. Foss also does some offshore towing for the Navy, including targets that are towed one and a half miles behind the tugs for obvious reasons.

Captain Ann Kinner

Captain Ann Kinner

There are tugboats and there are tow boats. Ann Kinner, US Coast Guard-licensed captain, operates the latter for TowBoatU.S., which is a bit like the AAA of the recreational boating community. Her boats, including the 24-foot *Reactor* on which we met, are berthed at one of San Diego's premier marinas, with easy access to fabled San Diego Bay and the Pacific Ocean beyond. *Responder*—four feet longer with twin diesels and more creature comforts—re-launched in April 2002, is now her primary long range vessel.

Captain Ann is in the rescue business and the territory she covers stretches one hundred miles south of Pt. Loma, including Ensanada, Mexico, north to Oceanside, California and one hundred miles offshore.

"Most of my work, however, takes place no more than five miles off Pt. Loma and, when the smaller fishing boats head out beginning in May, down towards the Coronado Islands. Inexperienced sailors who don't understand charts are good candidates for finding all the shallow spots. We are on the alert for ungroundings whenever the extreme low tides happen during the day, or when the popular anchorages are crowded and the last boat in sets the hook too close to the beach.

"The number one cause for engine failure seems to be overheating. Unwary vessels get themselves into the kelp beds and begin to suck that vegetation up into their cooling systems and, at some point, the engines get too hot and just stop running. The next most common problem seems to be electrical. The salt environment is very tough on wiring and can cause connections to break down, alternators to fail, which eventually leads to dead batteries because they weren't charging themselves as the skippers thought. If that happens and you're ready to move on or head home and your engine won't start, the next call from the cell phone is to our service.

"Of course there are all kinds of other mechanical problems, propellers that get wrapped with an unbelievable array of foreign matter, and for sailboats, weekend sailors who forget to reef their sails when it really starts to blow and get dismasted in the process."

Captain Ann grew up in Newport, Rhode Island, one of the world's premier sailing areas. She learned to sail on friends' boats and, like many Rhode Islanders, grew fond of living and working on the waterfront. She moved to California in the early 1970's, and, some 15 years later, found herself on the 14th floor of an office building in Costa Mesa, looking out at the Pacific Ocean and wondering to herself why she was in an office instead of out on the water.

"I made up my mind right then to get back into sailing, never wanting to have anything to do with the power or 'stink pot' boating community. So I joined a sailing club and soon became a member of the Coast Guard Auxiliary. There, I signed up for their search and rescue classes. It didn't take long to realize that, as a member of the USCG Auxiliary, I could go out on other people's boats as well. Eighty percent of the recreational vessels out there are power boats and I soon realized that they can be fun too and dropped my 'stink pot' bias.

"Five years ago I got my captain's license, and could begin to get paid for doing the boating work that I loved. I could teach on and/or about boats, could deliver boats, could find a job on the water. I said goodbye to the corporate world, gave the suits away, put the high heels aside, and started doing the kind of work I had grown to love. Now I live on a boat, own two boats—a 37-foot trawler and a 22-foot sailboat—and work right here on my fleet of red rescue boats. My life is the water—the water is my life.

"Often, we will reach a stricken vessel—wife and kids huddled aft and dad with that 'what have I done wrong' look about him—we may hear the wife say: 'Oh wow, they've sent such a small boat and it's being driven by a woman!' But once we've bundled the kids up in the sleeping bag for warmth, diagnosed the problem, re-started the engine or set up the tow line, the occupants begin to sense that things are going to be OK. Back at the dock or launch ramp, the smiles and thanks come pouring out."

Long Beach, California

Captain Rene Dominguez

Captain Rene Dominguez began working in the tugboat industry in 1957, when he was a young man in his early twenties. Like most sailors who build tugboat careers, he started as a deckhand—a job he performed well for more than ten years. Dominguez is the spitting image of a mariner who has worked on the water for 45 years. He is a bit portly, like me, with a full gray beard, like mine, yet he has a seaman's vocabulary and drawl that is uniquely his own. Born in Flagstaff, Arizona and raised in Spain until his family moved to San Pedro, California, when I visited he was just four days away from his official retirement from Foss Maritime and had become a legend on the Long Beach waterfront.

Capt. Rene Dominguez

"I started working for Crowley Marine—it was called Crowley Red Stack at the time—and was there for more than 20 years before joining Foss in 1978. I got my towboat operator's license in the late sixties and by 1972 received my license as a tugboat captain. For 45 years I worked this harbor, that is Long Beach and San Pedro, which are really two separate marine jurisdictions of about equal size. San Pedro is considered the Port of Los Angeles while, here in Long Beach, we are on our own. Of course a lot of the goods we move are destined for or come from Los Angeles as well. The Port of Long Beach, by the way, is ranked the eighth-busiest in the world and the second-busiest in the United States; and the container terminals in Long Beach and Los Angeles, ranked together, are third in the world after Hong Kong and Singapore."

According to the Port of Long Beach's statistics, the leading export commodities measured in bulk are petroleum and its ancillary products, chemicals, waste paper, foods, electric machinery and scrap metal. Leading imports are bulk petroleum, electric machinery, plastics, clothing and furniture.

Captain Charles Holmes

"From my earliest days at Crowley Marine, I worked only on single-screw tugs. When I joined Foss in 1978, I made the switch to the newer twin-screw boats. A few years later, in 1980, we received our first tractor tug, the Pacific Tractor. *My first ship-assist job as her captain was with a car carrier vessel, the* Don Juan. *I had a little trouble getting the tug to*

A Port of Long Beach pilot boat about to come alongside an inbound tanker soon to be moved from an outer anchorage to a more protected one so that "lightering" (offloading some of the cargo to lighters) can begin. This will reduce the draft of the tanker, enabling it to head for its designated berth.

the side of the ship, the whole tractor concept being so new to me, but I have since done more than 2,000 ship-assist jobs on tractor tugs. The incident reminded me of an earlier time when I was a fairly new captain. I had gone out to a ship, approached it and banged her pretty hard, backed off and came back only to hit her again. Finally the pilot on board the vessel used the radio and said, 'tell you what, Captain, just sit tight and we'll bring the ship to you!'

"Over my total career, just the jobs of which I have kept a record, number upwards of 26,000! One of those of which I am most proud, was assisting the Queen Mary, both when she entered the Port of Long Beach under her own power and later when she was shifted 'dead ship' to her current location. The Port of Long Beach has grown a great deal in recent years. Container traffic, inbound and outbound combined, has increased by 175 percent since 1990 and, taking statistics from that same year, the volume of all forms of cargo has increased by 50 percent. So we have been much busier recently than in my earlier tugboat years. My shipmates began calling me 'harbor maggot' a while ago because all of my work has been inside the harbor, never offshore."

Foss Maritime's newest tug, the *Marshall Foss*, is tied up alongside the barge that serves as headquarters for Foss' Long Beach operation. I am invited to board her as she is dispatched on a tanker escort mission. Just weeks after her official christening, she is under the command of Captain Charles Holmes. Rene Dominguez comes along for the ride, and there is no mistaking the nostalgic look in his eye as the tug gets underway on this beautiful Southern California afternoon.

We were outbound from Long Beach to meet the *Kliomar*, out of Limassol, Cyprus, and escort her move from an outer anchorage to a new spot inside the breakwater. There, some of her cargo of fuel will be offloaded by lighters before the ship proceeds to its fuel terminal dockage. This meant making up a line from the tug's bow to the tanker's stern so as to be able to help brake her or otherwise control her, should the ship itself lose power. This type of tanker escort is now required in some US ports by the United States Coast Guard for safety reasons. Captain Holmes, who has a long tugboat career and has been with Foss Maritime for about three years, explains:

"Our tug, the Marshall Foss, is a brand new 6,250HP, 98-foot-long and 40-foot beamed 'Azimuthing Stern Drive (ASD) Thruster Tug' built with an eye towards environmental friendliness to meet Southern California's stringent air quality standards. She is a very high powered boat with incredible maneuverability, both now necessary because the ships we assist, especially the very big tankers and the ever-larger container ships, demand those qualities.

"In more common, easier-to-understand language, the Marshall Foss is called a 'Z-Drive' tug, so-named because the drive shaft leading from the engines to the propellers follows a 'Z-like' path. The propellers are surrounded by a cylindrical tubing called a 'Kort Nozzle', named after Ludwig Kort, its German inventor, and attached to a vertical shaft that rotates a complete 360 degrees. Kort nozzle systems usually increase propulsion efficiency by 30% to 40% and are the state-of-the-art in tugboat propulsion. I can make this tug walk sideways, go backwards, turn completely around itself on a dime, all by moving the the 'joy sticks' on the controls. On many systems now the throttle and the turning controls are combined in one lever."

With afternoon shadows lengthening and the *Kliomar* safely at her new anchorage, we head back to the *Marshall Foss'* berth. The newest of the Long Beach/Los Angeles harbor tugs has performed another routine function well, and the legacies of Rene Dominguez and his colleagues seem ably passed on to Chuck Holmes and his current shipmates.

Underway to a calmer anchorage inside the breakwater, the tanker *Kliomar*, with a Cyprus registry, is tethered to Foss Maritime's tractor tug *Marshall Foss*. USCG regulations require this kind of tanker escort in several US ports so that the ships can be controlled and/or stopped should they develop engine problems or lose steerage.

Above, one of the Port of Long Beach's container terminals. Eighth-busiest in the world and second in the United States, the ports of Long Beach and San Pedro (Los Angeles' harbor) together are ranked third in the world after Hong Kong and Singapore.

Marshall Foss (right), Foss Maritime's recent California addition, provides welcome new muscle for the ports of Long Beach and San Pedro. On duty for more than a year now, *Marshall Foss* is 98 feet long with a 40-foot beam. Two Detroit Diesels provide 6,250HP and *Marshall Foss* develops a certified bollard pull rating of 83.3 tons.

Captain Carl Martin, Jr.

Captain Carl Martin, Jr.

Captain Carl Martin, Jr. grew up in Union City, New Jersey, across the river from the New York skyline, not too far from the banks of the Hudson where ships and barges made their home. After graduating from high school in 1977, he joined the US Navy.

"After boot camp, the Navy sent me to Portland, Oregon, where I was assigned to a destroyer, DD 718, the USS Hamner. I thought there must have been some mistake: the US Navy in Portland, Oregon? I told the taxi driver I needed to go to the US Navy Yard and he asked me if I was sure I was in the right town! We did find the ship, of course, which was used for Naval Reserve training. It was a big disappointment for me because I had thought I had joined the Navy to see the world, as the recruiting posters had claimed. And here I was on the Columbia River, 80 miles from the ocean, on a small insignificant naval vessel that trained civilian reservists."

This was the beginning of Martin's maritime career and an early exposure to the world of tugboats. The Columbia and Willamette Rivers in Portland are filled with workhorse boats that haul a variety of products including enormous quantities of grain and lumber, from as far away as Lewiston, Idaho, almost 400 miles up the river.

"I did get some sea time when the Navy transferred me to Mayport Naval Station in Jacksonville, Florida, and assigned me to a fast frigate, the USS Paul. We went to the Mediterranean twice and spent some time in the North Atlantic and the Caribbean. After the Navy, I returned to New Jersey where I worked for the US Postal Service for five years, hating every minute. Finally I was able to arrange for a transfer back to Portland. That is where I met my wife, a new love, and was reintroduced to the Columbia River, an old one.

"Soon I had joined a minesweeping unit of the Naval Reserve, stationed in Astoria, Oregon, at the mouth of the Columbia River. We had a 56-foot former fishing vessel that had been converted for use as a minesweeper. She had quite modern electronics on board and I was able to get some good navigating experience during that four-year tour between 1983 and 1987."

Crowley Marine has a Port of Los Angeles presence too. The "Red Stack Fleet," as they were once called, help move some of the 100 million tons of cargo handled annually in the ports of Long Beach and San Pedro.

Millennium Falcon, with 4400HP, is one of the Port of Los Angeles' most-powerful tugs. Millennium Maritime is a part of Harley Marine Services which operates 40+ vessels along the west coast of the United States.

Although postal work was his bread-and-butter day job, Captain Martin found himself in Astoria whenever he was free, especially on weekends. Soon, he met a man in his reserve unit, Justin Stoll, who was a tugboat captain working for the Shaver Transportation Company, one of Portland's largest and oldest marine towing firms. One of the company's most-respected captains, Stoll's recommendation carried a lot of weight and it didn't take long for Martin to land a job as a deckhand on a Knappton Towboat Company (now Foss Maritime) tug in Astoria. His days at the post office were over and his civilian maritime career had begun.

"We did all kinds of work. There was a good bit of ship assistance and we moved a lot of barges with containers towing them up river as far as Lewiston, Idaho, 450 miles from Astoria, and back down again. Many a grain barge was moved down river. We also did a lot of log-towing for the lumber industry and that included lots of walking on the logs, wearing those spiked boots. I had 13 years with Knappton/Foss and gained a wide range of experience."

Carl Martin is now the captain of the *Millennium Falcon*, a 105-foot Z-drive tractor tug, built in the year 2000 and berthed in San Pedro. With 4400HP, she is one of the most-powerful tugs in Los Angeles and Long Beach harbors. Millennium Maritime is a part of Harley Marine Services, which operates more than 40 vessels on the west coast of the United States. Its fleet of seven powerful tugs in Los Angeles and Long Beach harbors has quickly made its mark on the area and Captain Carl Martin is one of the reasons for the firm's success.

San Francisco, California

Captain Jeanne Pinto

Captain Jeanne Pinto

Growing up in Rhode Island, Jeanne Pinto has been immersed in boats all her life, as are many from this small coastal state. After moving west some 20 years ago, she started working in boat upkeep services, which led to a job painting two small ship-assist tugs in the San Francisco Bay area and riding along on some of their jobs.

"Here we were, going for a boat ride across the Bay, throwing a line up to a ship somewhere, pulling or pushing her wherever she needed to go, taking the line down and cruising to the next job. That sure seemed to beat the hours I spent sanding and scraping somebody else's boat!

"As I got to know the owner of a marine towing company better, I began to lobby him hard to hire me for some of the deck work on his boats. Owning my own business, the hours were quite flexible, so I could be available pretty much whenever the tug work needed to be done. The tug job was unionized and the pay was good in those days, though it's not any more, not having kept up with the enormous cost of living increases here in the Bay area.

"In the mid 1980s there was a labor strike here against Crowley Marine. That had a huge impact on the other, smaller San Francisco Bay companies because Crowley was the big player at the time. So companies like Oscar Niemeth Towing began working around the clock and needed to hire lots of extra hands. Oscar Niemeth himself still ran the company at that time and was thrilled to find a woman he could hire for his boats. He always said he felt that women paid so much more attention to detail and that they were cleaner too! So I joined the company, much to the chagrin of some of the men.

"I started with the company, running their oil-recovery vessel. It was a catamaran with a 25-foot tower for visibility. She was jet-powered with bow thrusters and steered terribly. Moving her was almost like sailing her. Here in the Bay tankers will often anchor and some of their cargo will be removed by lighters which come alongside the ship. By law an oil recovery vessel is required to stand by. We could be out there for long stretches of time—I think the longest was 72 hours straight—so you really had to like your shipmate a lot.

A Hapag-Lloyd container ship sails out to the Pacific Ocean underneath San Francisco's Golden Gate bridge. Sixteen million tons of cargo move in and out of Bay area ports each year.

Fortunately, my crewmate was a very likeable guy who loved to share stories.

"We would take turns standing watches and sleeping in the tiny two-foot berth. We had a refrigerator and a hot plate for meals and in the summer we would bring coolers with food and folding chairs—it would almost be fun. I had a 50-ton master's license, which allowed me to run this vessel. By working as a deckhand on the other tugs at the same time, I was able to accrue the hours necessary to upgrade, first to 500 and then 1600 tons."

The biggest weather factors in San Francisco Bay are wind and fog with the latter causing the most problems. But for the most part, weather doesn't affect ship-assist work here.

"So I've been lucky so far with my maritime experiences. The only semi-exciting story that comes to mind was the time we were towing a 300-foot-long mud scow down the Columbia River. The further downstream we moved, the worse the weather forecasts became with huge seas running 30 feet outside and the Columbia River Bar closed to vessel traffic. So we tied up at a dock and soon were called on the radio by a ship berthed near us, asking us, along with a Foss tug which was nearby, to hold her to the dock during the winds clocked at more than 100 miles, to keep her dock lines from parting. Evidently that had happened in an earlier storm and the ship that time was blown into the long bridge that spans the river between Oregon and Washington in Astoria. We came alongside and pushed for eight hours. The exciting part of the whole experience was watching the storm growing in intensity while we were safe in port."

Today Captain Pinto stays inside the Golden Gate during most of her on-duty time, moving ships in and out of San Francisco's seven-mile waterfront to and from the North Bay refineries and in and out of Oakland's ten container terminals. Along with San Pedro Bay near Los Angeles and Puget Sound in the Pacific Northwest, the San Francisco Bay area has become one of three principal Pacific Coast gateways for US containerized cargoes. Together, these three regions account for more than 40% of the nation's container cargo volume.

With its surrounding hills and valleys, San Francisco Bay's natural beauty makes it one of the most attractive places in the world. Driving a tugboat over its many square miles of water is not a bad way for a woman like Captain Jeanne Pinto to spend her days.

Tractor tugs of Baydelta Maritime, one of the Bay area's busy tugboat fleets, dockside at San Francisco's Pier 15.

Captain Joel Delizonna

I first spotted Westar's tug *Bearcat* circling in the waters just off San Francisco's Fisherman's Wharf, as she was waiting for her turn at a nearby fuel dock. Waving at her with my business card in hand, it didn't take long for the captain to nudge the boat over to where I was standing. The deckhand handed the card to the captain and I negotiated a meeting back at *Bearcat*'s home base, Pier 50 on the San Francisco waterfront, that evening. I arrived only to find Westar's offices closed, no *Bearcat* in sight.

Next morning, leaving early to catch a flight out of Oakland, I swung by Pier 50 again, just on the chance that the crew might be there. To my surprise, *Bearcat*'s Captain Joel Delizonna was there, pinch-hitting for the absent office receptionist. He was surprised and pleased to see me.

Westar Marine Services, with five launches and 14 tugboats, is one of the biggest marine towing companies in the San Francisco Bay area and Captain Delizonna has been working with them for ten years. He states:

"In addition to our present fleet, we have more boats coming. We do a little bit of everything: bridge work, construction, ship-assist, barge moves—matter of fact, Westar owns ten barges. We may not be the biggest company here in the Bay area—Foss, recently having added the AmNav fleet to its own, probably holds that title—but we are the most versatile.

"We're never on the same boat here at Westar, we run them all. The work changes every day, too. One hour we can be doing a ship job and then be assigned to tow a dump scow. You just never know. But most of our work is here, this side of the Golden Gate. Before joining the workboat industry, I fished for 15 years so I've had plenty of offshore experiences.

The "Cat 'n the Fiddle," name of a well known Sausalito, California restaurant, is also the name of the owner's live-aboard tug, berthed close by.

"Our launch fleet is under the sharp eye of Janis Smith and she is one of our captains as well. Janis has been with us for about three years now, starting out as a deckhand before she got her license. Our launches stay very busy, running ships' stores out to the vessels, doing pilot work when the pilots get swamped as they often do, working on our construction jobs, running crews back and forth."

Joel Delizonna has had his master's license for 24 years. For a long time he worked out of Half Moon Bay on party boats and fishing vessels, then came to San Francisco Bay some ten years ago. I asked him what he thought were some of the major challenges here on the Bay.

"I'd say wind, fog and the currents. You always have to plan according to those factors. When you have a fairly small boat pushing or towing a large barge and the currents are running three to four knots—five to six under the Golden Gate—and/or winds pick up, you have to choose and adjust your courses carefully if you don't want to completely blow your running times!"

Westar Marine Services was founded by Buzz Hefrin years ago with just a couple of tugs. Now the company is owned by his daughter Wendy and her husband, Dave Morrow, and by Mary McMillan and Bill Shurfee, also husband and wife. Westar's 14 tugs soon will be joined by number 15, now being built in Crescent City.

"Working for Westar is great. We are always upgrading our tugs, especially the power plants. We have more than 40 full-time employees with another 60 plus part-timers on call. For many of us who have spent long periods at sea, this is great work. Most of it is daytime duty, though you may not get home sometimes until ten at night. But at least you are home for most of the holidays and the birthdays and that's terrific for those of us with families!"

Above, Westar's tug *Bearcat* is one of a fleet of 14 tugs and 10 barges that makes this San Francisco marine towing firm one of the largest and most versatile in the San Francisco Bay area.

At right, a pilot boat heads towards a Port of Oakland container terminal in preparation for sailing a vessel that has finished loading. Container ships these days follow prescribed routings much like a land-based UPS truck and most often complete their unloading and loading operations within a 12-hour period, usually resulting in arrivals and departures on the same day.

The Tugboat *Robert Gray*

The tug *Robert Gray* was built for the US Army Corps of Engineers in 1936. With a beam of 26 feet and 118-feet-long, she draws 10 feet of water. *Robert Gray* was specifically constructed for use in Alaska, working as a research and surveying vessel and is still active in commercial work. Now based in the San Francisco Bay area, the tug is available for passenger cruising and other charter work, including voyages to and through Alaska's Inside Passage. For more information call 415-235-7878 (cell) or 415-512-7281 or visit the web site at: robertgraycharters.com. It's a great chance to sail on board a classic tug!

Other tugs are available in the Pacific Northwest for charter or for B&B accomodations.

The classic tug *Robert Gray* is available for overnight stays or long-term charters, especially to Alaskan waters.
You will call at ports like Ketchikan, Petersburg, Juneau, Haines and Skagway and transit the magical waters of the Inside Passage.

Captain Anthony Carter

Captain Tony Carter

Just back from a tow job that took boat and crew to Hawaii over a three-month period, the 125HP (that's right—125 HP) single-screw tug *Coast Pilot* rests comfortably at its berth at the northern end of San Francisco Bay in Richmond, California. Built in San Francisco in 1944, Captain Tony Carter is proud of the fact that she performed so well on her recent long open sea voyage.

Involved in boating all his life, Captain Carter moved to Santa Barbara, California from the Pacific Northwest in his early teens, finding his first tug job on board the *Rocket*.

"I got some early towing experience at that time, moving supplies out to the oil rigs and doing some tow work within the recreational-boating community as well. In the mid-sixties we formed Carter and Desmares, Inc. (CDI) here in the San Francisco Bay area, which provided general marine services to the Bay area, including towing and shipyard supervision.

"We became quite proficient at moving tugs destined for the Bay area from southern US Gulf of Mexico ports, transiting the Panama Canal, pulling payloads whenever we could find them. I was working with Jerry Morris at the time, who later owned Jericho Towing up in Petaluma. We bought several boats together including one from Foss maritime, the Mary Foss. Eventually, our company became quite good at long-haul towing, to places like Mexico and Ecuador, moving numerous dump scows and considerable quantities of construction equipment. Once we brought a 500 x 125-foot cement barge from Korea, where it was built, to a lagoon in Baja, California. Every job was a challenge and, in its own way, exciting!

"For a while our company was involved in a fishing operation off the coast of West Africa. Tow jobs took us to many places in North and South America and we did a lot of work for the United Fruit company, bringing supplies into Gulfito, Costa Rica. When the Sunshine Bridge in Tampa, Florida was hit by a ship and collapsed in the early 1980s, we towed the derrick needed to repair it from San Francisco to Tampa.

"In 1983 there was a dramatic drop in the price of crude oil and that put a lot of tugs, especially in the Gulf of Mexico, out of work. We had to tighten our belts too, realizing that the cream had gone out of the business. In those days there were quite a few independents like us, companies that owned four or five boats, and they really felt the economic impact. We ended up owning just Coast Pilot and a Miki tug because of their lower operating cost. By 1986 we were were forced to close CDI—but we were luckier than most, coming out of it with our skin and a few bucks."

For the next few years, Captain Carter did some charter work, going back to Central America, taking gold mining machinery to Costa Rica and discharging various cargo in the Gulf of Dulce. When asked about the history of his living aboard *Coast Pilot*, Carter responded:

"When the towing business declined severely, and about the time we sold the company, my wife and I began searching for an old wooden tug like this one to rebuild. One day a friend called to ask if we were still looking for a boat and told us about Coast Pilot, which was owned by Bank of America at the time. He described her as a 'piece of junk' and as a property that BA just did not want to own. The Boy Scouts of America had offered them a thousand dollars but the bank was a bit skittish about taking their money. Coast Pilot was laying in the Oakland Estuary at the time and had not seen a soul aboard her in at least six years. There were four feet of water in the engine room but she also had a carcass of an engine which I knew could bring me at least a few thousand dollars. So I doubled the Boy Scouts' offer to which the bank responded by saying that they had at least eight times that much in the project. My answer was, 'Hey, we are talking about my new mistake, not your old one!' When the banker still balked, I

asked him to call his corporate counsel and tell him about the four feet of water in the engine room and the several hundred gallons of fuel in the tanks—and then ask him what would the bank's liability be in such an instance? It didn't take very long before I owned a tugboat!

"At the same time I had made a commitment to bring a tug from Los Angeles to Juneau, Alaska. Just as we were starting to tear Coast Pilot *apart, they phoned and said they had one engine running and were down to three dock lines—so I flew down to LA on the next flight and started the voyage up the coast. When we were just about off of Eureka in northern California, my wife called and said 'I know you can't get off the boat now but, when you get to Tacoma, catch the next flight back because we are sinking!' Well, now the liability problem that I had flaunted before the bank was about to become mine! Fortunately, my wife recruited a bunch of our friends who kept the boat afloat and within a few hours of docking in Tacoma I was back aboard our vessel and had soon found and fixed the problem.*

"We worked on Coast Pilot *seven days a week for six years with a six-month interruption for some duty in Alaska at the time of the Valdez oil spill. Tug jobs came first until I was hired as a ship's surveyor—naturally, all the money earned went directly into* Coast Pilot's *resurrection. By the mid-nineties she had become a live aboard boat as well as a vessel that could do the occasional tow job, which still comes my way. We have towed a steamboat to Seattle and just came back from having towed a multi-million-dollar 90 x 20 foot houseboat to the port of Lahaina on the island of Maui in Hawaii. The voyage took us down to Los Angeles first to top off our fuel. We left there on Thanksgiving day, heading west towards Hawaii on a 17-day journey. The early weather wasn't terrific, with the boat rolling every few seconds, first 30 degrees to port and then to starboard. But we had an experienced towing crew, all buddies from previous times, and we cooked and ate a full Thanksgiving dinner even though it was a week late. The return trip lasted just 14 days. Under tow, heading west, we averaged 6.7 knots per hour while we did 7.1 knots on the way home.*

"We were the escort for the Bishop Museum's double hulled canoe Hukulea *on her coastwise voyage in 1995, probably our most fun trip. And* Coast Pilot *has been to Canada at least five times and to Mexico twice."*

Sitting in *Coast Pilot's* comfortable living quarters enjoying Captain Carter's fantastic coffee, I realized that he had created the best of all worlds for himself and his boat—establishing an on-the-water life that captures his love for the sea both professionally and recreationally. It's a model many others might want to emulate.

Coast Pilot, peacefully at home among her Richmond, California neighbors. The 125HP tug recently towed a 90 x 20-foot houseboat from California to the island of Maui, Hawaii.

Portland, Oregon

Captain Larry Johnson

Captain Larry Johnson

The Columbia/Snake River System ends at the Columbia River Bar, where the mighty waterway disgorges millions of tons of water into the Pacific Ocean every day. When the thunderous power of this river meets the Pacific, unpredictable and very dangerous sea conditions are created. These conditions are so perilous that it requires a designated group of ship pilots—the Columbia River Bar Pilots Association—to handle inbound and outbound ship traffic through that intersection. Once past the dangerous waters, inbound vessels are handed over to Columbia River Pilots, who continue to assist them as they head to or from the many ports that lie along the 85-mile stretch between Astoria, at the river's mouth, and Portland, Oregon.

Ocean-going vessels travel the Columbia River only as far as Portland, where cargo is transferred to barge tows for the rest of the journey as far as Lewiston, Idaho. The Columbia/Snake River System includes 36 ports in three states, 11 of them between Portland and Astoria, and serves over 40 states. It is the largest wheat transportation system in the United States, accounting for 43% of all US wheat exports in 2000 (courtesy of Columbia/Snake Marketing Group 2000) and is second to the Mississippi River in volume of total grain exports.

Captain Larry Johnson is Foss Maritime's Regional Director for its Columbia/Snake River Division. Having had a prior career in commercial fishing, he has been with Foss more than 20 years. Johnson came from Seattle to Portland four years ago to handle their large and varied Columbia/Snake River operations, which became Foss' fifth marine line of business. The other four divisions are: Pacific Northwest, San Francisco, Pacific Southwest and Ocean Transportation Marine. In addition, their three marine support operations are Foss Environmental, Foss shipyard and Ancillary Marine. Grain, forest products and containerized cargo are major river system commodities carried by Foss' new unit. (courtesy of Foss Maritime's 'A Living Legend')

"We are known as the Columbia/Snake River Division of Foss but we operate as far south as Los Angeles and as far north as Alaska. There are 16 tugs in our fleet here and 12 smaller vessels, mostly involved in logs and lumber, on Lake Coeur d'Alene in Idaho. In addition, we have more than 40 barges, including grain, fuel, container and even refrigerated container equipment."

Different from most west coast sea terminals, the Port of Portland is primarily an export harbor. According to MISER 2001 statistics, the value of Portland's exports increased by almost 30%, from $9 billion in 1998 to $11.4 billion two years later, making it the second-largest export tonnage port on the west coast.

"Logs and lumber used to represent one third of our export products here—but over the past four years, thanks to the influence that environmental concerns have had on the logging industry, that has dropped to zero. Today, 40% of the cargo is grain. We also move a lot of hay cubes and almost all of the french fried potatoes used by McDonalds worldwide. They come from Boise to Lewiston, Idaho by truck, are loaded on to barges for the downstream journey and then transloaded again here on to ships for export. There is a lot of concern among transportation people out here, mariners in particular, about the effect on our industry should the movement to eliminate some dams on the Columbia/ Snake River succeed. Advocates of breaching the dams claim that their presence impedes the salmon as they travel up river to spawn, resulting in a declining salmon population. But, historically, we have just experienced the two largest salmon breeding years ever recorded. That doesn't seem to stop the debate, which is still occurring. If the dams were breached, there would be a large loss of power for this part of the country. And every grain barge that could no longer transit the rivers would have to be replaced with 150 twenty-five ton semi-trailer trucks. To move the same amount of cargo currently

transported by barges on the Columbia/Snake River System annually would require 700,000 trucks or 125,000 rail car transits each year. In addition, Washington and Oregon are two of the most maritime-dependent states in the country with the marine industry accounting for one of every three jobs in Oregon.

"But aside from the economic impact of such a move, which would be huge, there are many environmental arguments that can be made in favor of water transportation. Though these comparisons have been put together by Columbia/Snake River Marketing, I believe them to be quite accurate. In terms of emission efficiencies by barging: hydrocarbon emissions: barge is 20% of rail and 14% of truck; carbon monoxide emissions: barge is 31% of rail and 11% of truck; nitrous oxide emissions: barge is 29% of rail and 5% of truck. In terms of fuel savings measured by the use of one gallon of fuel moving one ton of cargo: 514 miles by barge; 202 miles by rail; 59 miles by truck. Generally speaking, mariners appreciate clean waterways, which makes them pretty good environmentalists and we believe that the above factors are important parts of the overall focus on environmental protection. In terms of concerns on the waterway itself, the most important factor on the run to or from Lewiston or points between is the speed of the river. Though we had a bit of a drought in 2001, this year there has been quite a snow pack. That, combined with warmer temperatures which have brought an earlier snow melt, has caused the river to flow at speeds of seven to eight knots. Also, as the snow melts and fills up the areas behind the dams, they begin to release water through their spillways and that adds to water levels and current speeds.

Foss Maritime's push tug *Lewiston* on the Willamette River in Portland, Oregon. The Columbia/Snake River System of which the Willamette River in Portland is a part, covers some 450 miles from Lewiston, Idaho to Astoria, Oregon and includes 36 ports in three states.

Foss Maritime's Columbia/Snake River System operation includes 16 tugs, 12 smaller vessels involved mostly in logs and lumber, more than 40 barges including grain, fuel, container and refrigerated container equipment. Captain Larry Johnson supervises about 200 people. Moving cargo by barge is extremely fuel efficient One gallon of fuel will move one ton of cargo 514 miles by barge, 202 miles by rail and only 59 miles by truck.

"All the lock chambers on the Columbia/Snake River System are the same size and measure 86 x 650 feet. As a general rule, barges are built for the system and are 42 x 272 feet. A typical tow will consist of a push tug and four barges, which will just fit into the locks. We make the round trip to Lewiston two to three times a week with crews of four who stand six-on, six-off watches on a round trip that will typically take six days. Most of our people really like the work and stick around for a long time, which results in a very low personnel turnover rate of just about two percent, making the maritime industry here very mature. When you compare that to high technology, for instance, where employee turnover rates are measured in the 100+ percent range, you can appreciate the difference here."

In addition to river towing, Foss does offshore work as well.

"We used to ship a lot of chemicals, especially fertilizer, but in the last few years it has become cheaper to import it than to produce it here. The picture changes all the time, impacted by a variety of factors, some economic, some political. A strong US dollar makes it more expensive for others to buy US products, for instance; and the politics of any given time, domestically via price supports, might influence how much grain our farmers grow—while foreign policy frequently dictates how much of that same grain is exported as foreign aid. Sizeable amounts of grain leaves here and transits the Panama Canal for countries like Egypt."

Foss Maritime's Columbia/Snake River System operation employs some 200 people, all under the skillful direction of Larry Johnson. Although there are days when he would rather be on the tugboats themselves—moving away from the Willamette River docks that are home to Foss Maritime in this region, out to the Columbia River on a ship-assist or up towards Lewiston on a six-day tow—it's a job he loves and hopes to be able to fulfill for many years to come.

Captain Jeff Johnson

Captain Jeff Johnson

Shaver Transportation Company has been in the marine towing business since 1880, and is one of the major players in marine towing on the Portland, Oregon and Vancouver, Washington waterfronts, as well as along the entire route of the Columbia/ Snake River System, stretching for 450 miles from Lewiston, Idaho to Astoria, Oregon, at the mouth of the Columbia River.

As their brochure celebrating 100 years of service states, "If it's towing, Shaver does it, excelling in all forms of towing and harbor services such as ship-assist, grain and bulk commodity barging, general commodity barging and ocean towing. We are one of the few companies in the northwest that can pick up cargo in Pasco, Washington and deliver it to the Portland/Vancouver area from where it can be transloaded and shipped worldwide."

Captain Jeff Johnson came from an aluminum boat-building business in the Portland area 16 years ago to join Shaver Transportation. Like many tugboat sailors, he was preceded in the business by his father, a retired Columbia River pilot, who persuaded his son that working on the tugs on the Willamette and Columbia Rivers was not only an exciting and honorable career but a good way to earn a decent living. Actually, Jeff is a third-generation tug crewman—his grandfather worked on the tugboats too.

"Once you get your foot in the door at a company like Shaver, there is not a whole lot of turnover. I've had my captain's license for eight years now."

We are on our way down the Willamette River toward its intersection with the Columbia River to meet an incoming bulk carrier. The Port of Portland is the second-leading mineral

Shaver Transportation Company's twin-screw 3200HP tug *Vancouver* works ship-assists and barge tows on the Columbia, Willamette and Snake Rivers. Shaver Transportation calls itself "one of the few marine towing companies in the northwest that can pick up cargo in Pasco, Washington and deliver it to the Portland/ Vancouver area from where it can be transloaded and shipped worldwide.

bulk handling port on the west coast and the 670-foot-long *Paclogger* is inbound to receive just such a cargo at its terminal. Two other vessels, *Pan Pac Spirit* and *Forest Island*—both Panama registries—are already being loaded there.

With river pilot on board, *Paclogger* lifts anchor and starts moving upstream, slowly making the turn to starboard into the Willamette River. Jeff Johnson is in command of the Shaver tug *Vancouver* today, and the twin-screw 3200HP veteran responds with ease. Shaver's *Lassen* is the second boat on this ship-assist job. We pick up *Paclogger* on the fly on her port bow as we come alongside seamlessly—the ship line is hoisted up to the freighter's deck by means of a crane that is part of *Vancouver*'s equipment placed forward of the wheelhouse. *Lassen* makes up to *Paclogger*'s stern on her starboard side and, on the pilot's commands, the two tugs begin to turn her around in mid-stream. *Paclogger* is eased towards the berth on her starboard side with a gentleness that reflects the many years of docking experience of the pilot and both tugboat captains.

By no means are we the only activity on the Willamette this afternoon. Other Foss, Crowley and Shaver tugs have been moving petroleum and bulk barges up and down the river while a large automobile carrier, freshly emptied of its cargo, moves smartly downstream under its own power.

For Captain Jeff Johnson and Shaver Transportation, it's another day on the river, keeping America's exports and imports flowing smoothly. These river mariners make it look so easy. But knowing the river's twists and turns, its currents, sandbars, and moods on any given day is anything but easy and requires the knowledge that comes from what these crews experience day in and out. Only by multiplying that experience by the thousands of miles of US waterways, and the thousands of offshore miles covered by other sailors every day, do we begin to appreciate these men and women who perform 24/7, foregoing family birthdays and traditional holidays.

Without these marine towing companies and their tugboat crews, ours would be a very different world.

As the *Vancouver* works the port bow of the 670-foot bulk freighter *Paclogger*, Shaver Transportation's tug *Lassen* handles the freighter's port quarter. *Vancouver* carries a crane just forward of the pilot house that can actually lift a ship's line to the vessels it is assisting, a labor-saving device for its deckhands! The Port of Portland is the second leading bulk handling port on the west coast.

The *Columbia*, a retired lightship, is now a part of Astoria's new maritime museum. A large sea buoy is in the foreground.

Tacoma, Washington

Captain Shawn O'Connor

Captain Shawn O'Connor

"We crew up at 0600. Be there if you want to come along."

The words of Captain Shawn O'Connor, who would skipper the 48-foot, 365HP Foss tug *Lela Foss* in Tacoma, Washington this morning, were plenty strong enough to get me out of bed three hours earlier for the drive south from Seattle on Interstate 5.

The $19.8 billion in foreign waterborne trade that moved through the Port of Tacoma in the year 2000 made it the tenth-largest trading port in the United States. I was excited at the prospect of being on its waters. Tacoma is especially attractive for another reason—it is the place where Foss Maritime began in the summer of 1889, when Norwegian immigrant and founder Thea Foss purchased a used rowboat for five dollars so that she could supplement the income earned by her carpenter husband, Andrew. Their's is a quintessential story of immigrants coming to the United States, working hard to gain a foothold in their new homeland and who, through a combination of hard work and good business sense, began building companies in many industries that helped propel this country into a position of global economic leadership.

Company history states that Thea Foss "spruced up her rowboat with green and white paint—still Foss Maritime's colors to this day—and sold it for a profit." She soon bought and sold other rowboats and, before long, earned enough money to begin keeping the boats that her husband was now building. Eventually, the Foss family had a flourishing boat-rental business at Twelfth and Dock Streets in Tacoma. Painting "Always Ready" on the roof of their boathouse, Thea established the firm's motto, which is still their claim to this day. Their three sons—Arthur, Wedell and Henry—and Andrew's brothers, Iver and Peter, all helped to make the business grow. City Waterway in Tacoma's harbor, so called because of its downtown location, was renamed Thea Foss Waterway in honor of the Foss founder, during the company's centennial celebration in 1989.

Now, well into its second century and its 114th year of continuous service, Foss Maritime and its fleet of tugboats and barges is one of the major players in the towboat industry up and down the US west coast, still green and white in color, with "Always Ready" splashed in red on the company's logo. Anywhere equipment or cargo needs to be moved on the water in the west, Foss vessels will be there, building on a very proud tradition that began with a five-dollar rowboat.

The early morning mist is beginning to burn off the port of Tacoma's waters as Captain O'Connor guides *Lela Foss* to the day's first assignment—moving logs closer to the loading log

One entire waterway in the Port of Tacoma is dedicated to the lumber industry.

carrier *Aries Harmony*. The logs had been moved away from the ship the night before so that a bunker barge could be brought alongside to fuel the vessel. Now they have to be returned to the ship's side in order for its cranes to begin loading again. We are moving towards the ship berthed about a mile up the waterway, as the captain explains the log raft sections that are in the water.

"The outside logs are called 'boom sticks' and measure 60 feet in length. Each log raft will have six sections in it and will be bordered by 14 boom sticks. Inside the boom sticks are the 'truckloads' of logs which we call bundles and there will be 60 to 70 such truckloads in a six-section raft. The bundles vary in size, from 20 to 40 logs each, depending on log size. Each raft will keep 60 or 70 logging trucks off the road and the economy of scale there is that one ton of waterborne cargo can move over 500 miles on one gallon of fuel while that same ton can move only 59 miles by truck on that same gallon—a fuel savings of approximately ten to one. (courtesy of Columbia/Snake River Marketing Group). So shipping the logs from Everett or Port Angeles, Washington, or even from Canada, to the Port of Tacoma in the water is considerably cheaper than moving them by truck. Even barges are now being used more often to ship the logs down here as a preference over trucks.

"A typical Weyerhauser log ship will load five rafts directly from the water and then will top off their holds with another 1,000 bundles. When fully loaded, they will be carrying 5.2 to 5.4 million board feet of logs and, though we used to get more, we now average four such ships each month. In the really busy times of the 1970's and 1980's, we would have that number of ships in a week. That will give you an idea of how diminished the timber industry has become.

Omer Foss in the midst of logs destined for the Simpson Lumber Mill, largest in the United States.

"I call this a 'Weyerhauser' vessel because of the logs it carries. It is actually owned by a Japanese company by name of 'Kawasho.' They will send their wood buyers to this area who will then select certain woods from what they see—then they will order two million board feet of a certain type or quality, one million board feet of something else and so on, until they have a ship load. Then they will order the ship to Tacoma and it will be loaded with the requested logs. The logs for export are almost always the best, top-of-the-line quality. Most of the logs in the water in Tacoma at the moment are probably destined for domestic consumption—there are a number of sawmill operations here, including Simpson Mill, the largest in the United States. Some are so sophisticated that they have computers that will take a picture of a log, determine the best cuts to get out of it—i.e. three two-by-fours, one two-by-six, etc.—and will then direct the cutting machinery to treat the log accordingly."

Shawn O'Connor was in high school when he started working on tugboats.

"I was working at a local gas station knowing that I wasn't going to pump gas the rest of my life when, one day, a couple of tugboaters came in to fill up. We started talking and they gave me their business card, suggesting that I come in to speak with one of their people. It turned out that he was a friend of my brother's and he hired me on the spot. I started working for Dunlap Towing in 1979 when I was 17. I've never regretted that decision.

"When Dunlap left Tacoma harbor I worked for their outside division and sailed to Hawaii for a year on trips that averaged 54 days. We would sail from Seattle to Oakland to Long Beach, California, then west to Honolulu where about half the cargo would be offloaded. The rest would be dispersed on an inter-island run that would take about five days, then back to Honolulu for additional cargo or empty containers to take back to Seattle. We would be home about ten days, then turn around and do it again. After Hawaii I sailed to Alaska for a year and a half.

"Ken and I currently work 12-hour days for 15 days a month. Soon we will start a new schedule that calls for 21 days on-call out of which we will work 15 and have an assigned seven days each month off."

A former Soviet Foxtrot class submarine, recently brought to the Port of Tacoma as a tourist attraction.

Ken Kovatch is working the deck on *Lela Foss* today, which means that he comes equipped with fairly warm outer gear and heavy, spiked rubber boots for walking on the logs that they'll be shifting during this long work day. His marine activities started at age 18 with a three-year Navy enlistment from which he went directly into the Merchant Marine where he obtained his AB ticket. By 1987, he was working for Crowley Maritime and then Seacoast Maritime before coming to Foss on April 1, 1989. Six years ago he obtained his captain's license, but today he is the deckhand.

It's a role he plays well when, by mid-morning, *Lela Foss* and *Omer Foss* are requested to unravel a bunch of boom sticks that were scheduled to be moved down harbor to a holding area. The sticks' chains, which tie them together so they can form the perimeters for the log rafts, had become quite tangled and it took a lot of hard work on the logs to straighten them out.

I wanted to know what an ocean log tow was like so Captain O'Connor related the following story:

"We were up in Port Angeles, Washington, getting a raft ready for towing. You would always go out to Morris Creek and Green Point, some seven miles outside of Port Angeles, to check the weather. Green Point has a very shallow bottom which causes swells, wind or not, and if we would find swells we would turn around and wait for the next tide change. When you are towing logs like that, you are very dependent on the tides. You would try to leave Port Angeles at the end of an ebb tide and try to catch the flood tide so that it would push you and give you that first jump which would take you to Dungeness, then to Point Wilson and into Port Townsend. You would wait there for the following tide. When towing logs like that, you are only making one and a half to two knots headway, so the push you get from the tides is important because it will give you an extra knot or two to

The log carrier *Aries Harmony* at work loading logs right out of the water. When ready to sail for Japan, she will have 5.4 million board feet of logs in her holds. Though traffic used to be higher, an average of four such vessels now call at the Port of Tacoma each month.

Bordered by 60-foot-long "boom sticks," each log raft will have six sections in it, surrounded by 14 boom sticks. A six-section log raft will contain 60–70 truck-loads (bundles) of logs. The bundles contain 20–40 logs each, depending on size.

get going—absent that push you go backwards, which is not fun. On one of these runs we were coming around Marrowstone Island, heading down Puget Sound and I had just come on watch as we literally came to a screeching halt! We had a flood tide with which we should have been some eight miles farther south than we actually were but, for some reason, we just were stopped. It was as though something had reached out from the floor of the Sound and grabbed our hull. We never could explain it.

"In a scenario that was just the opposite, another tug left Port Angeles with a log raft tow and found itself in a flood tide so strong that it pushed them all the way to Port Townsend in just one jump. When daylight broke they found that they only had four bundles left in their raft and nothing but sticks in the water. Somehow it all had come undone, which is why they went so far on that single jump. Losing your tow is no fun either."

By the end of the morning, we had sailed by a former *Foxtrot* Class Soviet submarine which had recently come to Tacoma under new ownership. It is scheduled to become a tourist attraction in the harbor—a duty far less dangerous than its original assignment. After watching two other Foss tractor tugs spin an incoming container ship around in the harbor so that it could be backed into its waterway for docking, Captains O'Connor and Kovatch brought *Lela Foss* back to its home base. There, I would disembark as they took a short break before heading for their next job. I had learned a lot about the Port of Tacoma and the important role that the logging industry plays within it.

Above, *Lela Foss*, single-screw 365HP tug, is assigned mostly to lumber work. Here she takes a short break in mid-morning, having been underway since 0600. Her two-person crew works 21 days on call out of which 15 will be on the water; seven off days will be assigned each month.

Though Ken Kovatch (right) also has a captain's license, he is the deckhand today, spiked rubber boots and warm outer gear an important part of his clothing.

Seattle, Washington

Fremont Tugboat Company

Captain Tom Bulson

Captain Erik Freeman

Margie and Mark Freeman were coming across Seattle's Lake Union from their houseboat on the opposite shore when I first spotted them waving. I was aboard the Fremont Tugboat Company's tug *Sovereign*, ready to observe a ship-shifting job on which they were about to embark.

Erik Freeman and Tom Bulson are *Sovereign*'s crew today. Friends since junior high school, the two young men own Fremont Tugboat Company now, while Mark and Margie are still responsible for the marina end of the business. *Sovereign* is a 660HP twin-screw tug built in 1943. She has a wooden hull and a steel house, and joined the Fremont fleet when Mark Freeman won second prize in the State of Washington's first lottery.

Tom joined Fremont 11 years ago, after some construction time and five years in commercial fishing on seine boats in Southeast Alaska.

"I love being here because our work presents different challenges almost every day. And I get to go home every night, though we are on 24-hour call."

In addition to their tugboating, Fremont is also the Seattle representative of TowBoatU.S., the emergency tow service for the recreational boating community. The rescue aspect of their workload increases dramatically as the summer yachting season begins. But rescues are not limited to summer and do not always involve boats on open water. In late May 2002, a major fire swept a Lake Union marina just around the bend from Fremont Tugboats. Excerpts from Mark Freeman's June 2002 newsletter reported their response:

"The type of smoke was a dead give-away for oil, gas and fiberglass—which means boats on fire. We alert Captain Erik on the Nextel, throw on some gear for a cold night on the water. As we round the cape on our 15-foot tug Jeep *we see that the fire is at the Seattle Marina and it is far worse than we had expected. After staring, stunned, for several seconds we get the word from the Fire Department to start pulling yachts away from their docks out to open water. Margie and I start in on the outside boat,* Show Me the Money, *about 65-feet long. Someone else had tied a sailboat onto the big yacht and we actually get two boats out on the first tow. Smoke, ash and falling debris are everywhere. As we hand the first two boats off to folks on small inflatables, Captains Erik and Tom show up with tugs* Stinger *and* Standfast *respectively. All in all, the four of us saved five powerboats, one sailboat plus one huge Boston Whaler. This fire produced a real community effort to fight it. I have never seen so much assistance from the public, helping those brave folks in charge. It took all of us to make the difference."*

Erik Freeman grew up on the water and continued in the business that his grandfather, "Doc" Freeman, and then his father, Mark, owned. He has been driving his own boats through these waters since he was eight years old. Now a partner in the tugboat business with his old friend Tom, and a new father himself, Erik knows the Seattle towboat business inside and out. He goes about it with a methodical professionalism that is impressive. He and Tom switch roles every day so that one will skipper the tug while the other will be the deckhand. Today it is Erik's turn on deck while Tom is in the wheelhouse. "We never get bored this way", they say simultaneously.

The *Capelin*, a Western Pioneer freight boat, needs to be moved from Lake Union Drydock to the Western Pioneer yard in Salmon Bay. At just under 200 tons and 180-feet long, she used to haul freight up and down the Inside Passage in Southeast Alaska.

Sovereign eases up to *Capelin* so that Erik can board the ship to determine the best way to tow her. Mark Freeman stands by on *Stinger*, its bow pressed to the side of the bigger ship, awaiting instructions. All three crewmen are in steady communication via two-way radios and the crisp preciseness of their words helps make this a very smooth job. Erik determines how to secure the line, and *Sovereign*'s port bow makes up to *Capelin*'s starboard side, astern of

Margie and Mark Freeman are legends on the Seattle waterfront. Fremont Tug, founded by Mark's dad, is now owned by his son Erik and Tom Bulson. But the Freemans own and operate Fremont Boat, a marina offering a good home to many a Seattle boat owner. Most days Mark will be on the water aboard *Stinger*, a launch/tug, helping Erik and Tom. Unless, of course, the Freeman's are sailing Alaskan waters in their beautifully reconditioned former USCG Buoy Tender, *Blueberry*.

Fremont Tugboat Company's tug *Standfast*, docked at Fremont Boat's marina on the Lake Washington Ship Canal.

amidships, and the tug slowly begins to ease the bigger ship away from the Crowley Maritime tug to which she has been rafted.

As is often the case, factors unrelated to the two vessels need to be considered for this move. Today's problem is not tides, winds or currents, but opening time for the Ballard Bridge over the Ship Canal, which will be closed for repair for most of the coming year (its first major overhaul since 1916). Half-leaf openings are available on demand except for normal closed periods. Two-leaf openings, which *Sovereign* alongside *Capelin* will require, occur only at 0500, 1100 and 1900. Captain Tom shoots for the 1100 opening and makes it through. *Capelin*'s new home is just another half-hour down the canal.

When we return to *Sovereign*'s home port at the Fremont's marina, we tie up to *Standfast* and spin her around so that we are directly on the dock. Then I am introduced to Mark's extensive and impressive museum collection of photographs (he keeps a camera on each tug) and models, mostly built by him. As we pour over the collection, Mark shares his family's incredible marine history with us. May Fitzpatrick had just graduated with a business degree from the University of Washington in the late 1920s and was working at the Seattle Hardware Company when a man entered the store saying, "Hi, I'm Doc Freeman." Though her immediate response was "who cares," it was the beginning of a romance that lasted 37 years until Doc Freeman's death in 1963. He bought and sold more than 1,000 boats during that time and left behind a shining reputation as a good and successful businessman. Together, May and Doc survived the depression years when a five-dollar check for moorage gave them food money for a week.

With a wide smile, Mark, now in his late sixties, retells the story. His wife, Margie, chuckles as the tale unfolds.

"We always lived on the water. During the Second World War, hundreds of Navy minesweepers, tugs and cargo ships were serviced by our shop. Dad bought dozens of

Above, *Stinger*, with Mark Freeman at the helm, moves past Western Towboat's fleet on the Lake Washington Ship Canal.

Erik Freeman and Tom Bulson alternate their roles at Fremont Tug on a daily basis—deckhand one day, captain the next. Here Erik reaches the dock prior to boarding the *Capelin*, a Western Pioneer freight boat dead in the water, prior to shifting her from the Lake Union Drydock to the Western Pioneer yard in Salmon Bay.

landing barges after the war and my job was to come home from school and pump those boats out until I dropped. I always thought I would die with a scow pump starter rope in my hand!"

At 13, Mark bought his first tug, the *Seal Rock*, borrowing $650 from his parents, which he paid back by salvaging logs from the water. Three years later, he bought his second tug, *Jerkmore*, for $2,500. In 1955 he began a four-year hitch in the US Coast Guard and, while stationed at the Grays Harbor Lifeboat Station in Westport, Washington, saved 37 lives during that tour as certified by an official US Coast Guard memorandum. It was a very unusual record. Returning to Lake Union in 1959, Mark bought the company back from the two employees to whom Doc Freeman had sold it. He quit selling boats in 1963 because he just did not like sales and concentrated on mooring and towing—both family businesses still thriving to this day.

On 24-hour call since that day in 1959 until the time that Erik and Tom took charge of the towing end of the business, Mark and Margie now can enjoy occasional breaks from Lake Union waters on their converted USCG buoy tender *Blueberry*. Designed for work on the Columbia River, which meant being able to handle rapids with currents up to 12 knots, *Blueberry* was built by Birchfield Boiler and Shipbuilding Corporation in Tacoma, Washington and was launched during the fateful month of December, 1941. By the following February, drawing only four feet of water and displacing just 39 gross tons, she was working the upper Columbia River.

Known then as CG 521 and configured as a push tug, *Blueberry* nosed a construction barge up and down the Columbia River for most of her life. Many a beacon, tower, range marker and river buoy were sited from that barge or hauled up onto it for maintenance and repair. CG 521 did her work on the river well for more than 30 years. She was bought and fitted for civilian life by Peter Whittler of Orcas Island, a man who liked and respected the gutsy, military craft. When the Freemans first boarded her in 1984, it was love at first sight, and Mark knew that he would buy her if ever he could. Some seven years ago that dream came true and, after some more of Mark and Margie's TLC, *Blueberry* has become the cruising boat they wanted while retaining enough workboat characteristics—extra fendering, tow bitts, towing lights, small crane, firefighting gun, etc.—to also be a part of their working tug fleet. The Coast Guard's motto *"semper paratus"* (always ready) is a part of the boat's soul and reflects Mark's love for the service to which he was so dedicated.

Starting with Orrin "Doc" Freeman's dogged determination to shape a mariner's life right along with his spunky wife, May, the Freeman family has become a legend on the Seattle waterfront. Handed down first to Mark, and now to Erik and his partner—childhood friend Tom Bulson—Fremont Tugboat Company's long history has become part of the lore of the marine industry in the Pacific Northwest.

Now that Erik and his wife Heidi have a new addition to the family, it may very well be that Marina May Freeman is already being groomed as another of Doc Freeman's successors. Many sunrises and sunsets will pass before she gets her captain's license (as she undoubtedly will). But when she does, it is not too hard to imagine her joining the ranks of women captains in the US tugboat fleet, moving smartly into or out of the Ballard Locks on that day's mission.

(opposite, top) Mark Freeman on *Stinger* gets ready to shift the *Capelin* on orders from Capt. Bulson. *Capelin* used to ply Alaskan waters bringing freight north from the Seattle area.

(opposite, bottom) A Foss Maritime tug has just pulled the container ship *Direct Eagle* out of the Duwamish River into Seattle's Elliot Bay as she starts her voyage north on Puget Sound.

Alaska

One Thousand Miles to Skagway

Captain Mike Wark

I am aboard *Western Titan* as she moves slowly but purposefully down Seattle's Lake Washington Ship Canal on a flawless September afternoon. We pass the tangle of hulls, stacks, masts, docks and mariners that are the guts and soul of Seattle's commercial fishing community and ease gently into the Ballard Locks. Not a single person there to watch our 20-foot descent towards the salt water of Puget Sound would guess that this handsome and scrappy Seattle tugboat, part of Western Towboat Company's fleet, is about to depart on a 2,000-mile journey to Southeast Alaska and back. Skagway, the northernmost point on the Inside Passage, will be her turn-around port. Every other Wednesday, she proudly and effortlessly makes this journey under the guidance of her highly professional and experienced crew.

Western Towboat was founded by Bob Shrewsbury in 1948 with just one boat and a promise to his customers that he would offer them "the best service possible along with his personal hands-on approach to marine towing." Since taking the helm, sons Bob, Jr. and Ric have grown the company enormously without changing a word of their father's commitment to excellence.

Our skipper on this day in September, 2002 is Captain Mike Wark, who has been with the company for 14 years and previously served in the USCG and captained smaller passenger vessels in Alaska, Panama, and Tahiti. First Mate Eric Bevans is an 11-year veteran of this fleet—a drummer in a rock band in his earlier years. Terry Waldal is our second mate (and great cook). With Western Towboat for 13 years, Terry came with mate's experience, having worked on a catamaran barracks boat in Alaska that housed cleanup crews during the time of the Valdez oil spill. AB Tyler Peterson, new kid on the block with only six months on the job, is an experienced Alaskan fishing captain who accrued his knowledge of Alaskan waters over a period of a dozen years. The squint of his eyes reflects the fierceness of the Bering Sea, where he had so often fished.

Western Titan is a five-year-old tractor tug—a 110' long workhorse whose two Caterpillar 16-cylinder "V" diesels develop 4200HP. She and her *Titan* class sisters are well known within the US marine industry as the only Z-drive tractor tugs used in long-haul towing applications. The Ulstein Z-drive technology used brings the power from the engine aft via a drive shaft, then vertically down through the hull via a drive leg, then horizontally again via the propeller shaft to the propellers housed in their Kort nozzles. The lower leg rotates 360 degrees, replacing rudders for steering. It's a technology that makes docking the freight barges at their Alaskan terminals an easier, faster and safer operation.

Foss Maritime tug and tow are rainbow blessed on Seattle area waters.

We arrive at the Alaskan Marine Lines terminal on the Duwamish River at 1745. Founded by Bob "Senior" and two other men in 1976 as "Southeast Barge Lines," Western Towboat actually ran the freight service for four years. Now owned by the Lyndon Family of Companies, AML promises scheduled freight service to dozens of Alaskan cities, knowing that as long as they can provide the terminals, equipment, and processes needed to handle the freight, Western Towboat will provide the tugs needed to get barges to their destinations safely and on time. Without a system of surface roads and with the exception of a few items brought in by air, most southeastern Alaskan communities are totally dependent on waterborne freight for everything from toothpicks to gasoline, groceries to building materials. The tugs and their tows meet their sailing schedules throughout the year, regardless of weather, with very few exceptions. It is a business relationship unusual in its efficiency and amicability.

Tongass Provider, the 320' x 94' deck barge that is our tow, is ready to sail at 1800, loaded with 365 TEU's (twenty-foot equivalent units). Western Towboat's harbor tug *Westrac* makes up to the barge's stern while Captain Wark positions *Western Titan* at her bow. The heavy chains that form *Tongass Provider*'s bridle are connected to the tug's towing cable via a fishplate and "D" shackles and we are off, bow pointing north up Elliot Bay and then Puget Sound. I had often watched marine traffic enter or depart the Port of Seattle. Now *Western Titan* and her tow were the departees and I was aboard, feeling the synergy between self and sea that has always existed. Many of the land masses we would pass and the bodies of water we would cross in the days ahead bore the names of the mariners who accompanied British Captain George Vancouver as his expedition charted these waters in 1792—Vancouver Island, Cape Mudge, Whidby Island, Mt. Baker, Puget Sound, Menzies Bay, to name a few.

Early evening gives way to dusk, then dark, as we move past Whidby Island to starboard—the barge about 1,000 feet astern. Watch schedules have been assigned for the 65-hour trip to

Western Towboat's *Western Titan*—five years old, 110 feet in length, with two 16-cylinder Caterpillar diesels providing a 4200HP rating. Every Wednesday and Friday, Western Towboat tugs leave Seattle towing container barges to Southeastern Alaska.

Ketchikan—our first stop. Since Western Towboat crews are unique in that they load and unload the barges at the Alaskan ports, receiving supplemental hourly pay for this work—these watches are dependent on arrival and departure times. As Captain Wark says,

"From the moment we leave the dock in Seattle, every decision I make is made with the goal of returning as quickly as possible. That's good for our families, because we sail every other Wednesday, no matter when we return, and for the company in terms of fuel and payroll savings. However, we never sacrifice safety in that process."

The first of many sumptuous meals is served in *Western Titan*'s large and immaculate stainless steel galley. Other tugs are pulling or pushing other tows on US waters this very moment, all contributing to the domestic waterborne freight moved on US waterways, one billion tons in the year 2000 (the last available year of record). That statistic, collected and analyzed by the US Army Corps of Engineers, compares to 1.4 billion tons imported or exported, and underscores the real importance of the towboat industry and the amount of domestic freight that it carries, all made possible by the American tugboat community.

Of the 365 TEU's aboard *Tongass Provider*, (there would be 550 on the return trip), 60 were reefers that contained perishable freight. These are checked once a day to make sure that the generators on the barge that provide the power are working properly. To get crew members aboard the barge, *Western Titan* veers to port and allows *Tongass Provider* to catch up with it, then eases up to come alongside and make the transfer. She then moves out ahead again to full wire, until the checking is done and the crew needs to be retrieved. Though a very easy and smooth operation on our trip, this gets a little less comfortable in winter weather.

In these Canadian waters as in most U.S. jurisdictions, Vessel Traffic System (VTS) controls marine traffic much like air traffic controllers do—vessels report in at major points giving their name, direction and ETA for the next landmark. This takes on special import at narrow sections along the Inside Passage like Seymour Narrows, where tug captains pulling tows are loathe to meet oncoming traffic, especially deep-draft cruise ships.

Though seas on the Inside Passage are, for the most part, fairly calm, there are three passages open to the Pacific Ocean; Queen Charlotte Sound, Dixon Entrance and Millbanke Sound all can create very nasty sea conditions, sometimes so severe that tugs and tows delay their crossings until conditions improve. But today, skies are mostly blue, with just enough clouds of varying shapes and color to add excitement to the bold green mountain landscape that spreads in all directions as it spills down to meet the water whose depths generally measure in the hundreds of fathoms.

Were we a bit closer to shore, the evergreens cascading to the water's edge would be more inclined to take on their individual personalities of Douglas Fir, Hemlock, Sitka Spruce, Western Red Cedar. And the beaches towards which they grow might host a grizzly or two, some Sitka black-tailed deer or a family of black bears. Other days, the dark green waters might show off a humpback or an orca whale. On this trip, a flotilla of porpoises in their torpedo-shaped, muscular bodies race along *Western Titan*'s bow playing their games of hide-and-go-seek, which they always win.

We reach Ketchikan on the third day. Petersburg (where some freight destined for more western ports will be

Western Towboat's harbor tug *Westrac* heads for home after pulling the container barge *Tongass Provider* off her Duwamish River Alaska Marine Lines dock.

Alaska Marine Lines'
barge *Tongass Provider*
(above) on waters of
Alaska's Inside Passage.
Alaska Marine Lines pro-
vides regularly sched-
uled twice weekly
freight service to many
Southeastern Alaskan
communities, the only
way, except for small
amounts of air freight,
these cities and towns
can receive the goods
their populations need
for their daily lives. The
barge can carry as many
as 600 TEU containers
stacked five stories high!

The *Western Titan*
(right).

Western Towboat launches another *Titan* class tug. The company builds its own vessels in its yard at company headquarters, right on the Lake Washington Ship Canal. They average a new boat every 15 months. Each new *Titan* tug incorporates design changes that are the result of the experiences of Western Towboat crews and the marine towing industry.

transloaded), Juneau and Haines are all about 10–11 hours apart. Skagway, just a few hours farther, was once a roaring gold-rush community where one provisioned before heading for the Yukon Territory—and where the winners were celebrated and the losers were nursed. At 0200, its streets are empty, the only sounds coming from the forklifts on board *Tongass Provider*.

Within five minutes of arrival in each port, after a docking so gentle you could put a dozen eggs on any galley surface and not break a single one, the unloading and loading begins, and *Western Titan* will always sail within five minutes of its crew having completed that work. Finishing in Skagway, there is a discernible upbeat feeling amongst the crew because now they know they're heading home.

The last stop southbound in Ketchikan will pose a special loading challenge for the skipper, for here the placement of the freight becomes critical and three issues are of greatest importance. One is the weight distribution on the barge, so that *Tongass Provider* rides evenly from a side to side perspective. Secondly, we need greater weight concentration towards the stern, forcing the bow upwards, creating what tugboaters call "rake." On this trip, the bow will ride up three feet, resulting in much easier control and steerage for *Western Titan*'s helmsmen. Finally, reefers have to be in as close proximity to each other as possible for the shortest possible electrical connections between them and the generators. Our containers are now stacked five high, as tall as a five-story building, and are lashed securely with chains to prevent slipping or sliding at sea.

By 0600 of our tenth day, Mt. Rainier is silhouetted ahead of us by a brightening sky as we re-enter Seattle's Elliot Bay. The *K&A*, a bulker on her way to Tacoma, slides by to port, while the container ship *CSX Tacoma* comes towards us, and the well-lit cruise ship *Amsterdam* heads for Seattle's Pier 66. Captain Wark appears in the wheelhouse to prepare for his Duwamish River landing. Wark, Bevans, and Peterson, after getting *Western Titan* back to her Ballard dock, will have four days off before they have to sail again. Terry Waldal will skip the next trip for his 20th high school reunion. No one is sure how well his replacement can cook.

(above) With the Port of Prince Rupert, British Columbia, Canada, far off our port bow, we cross the waters known as Dixon Entrance on our way south, back to Seattle. This incredible sunset provided 60 minutes of oranges and purples that played escort to the fireball of the sun as it slipped below the western horizon. Open to the Pacific Ocean, these waters can be roiling at times—but this day the seas were calm as time seemed to freeze in the midst of such unusual beauty.

(right) Western Towboat's home base on Seattle's Lake Washington Ship Canal.

Acknowledgments

Special thanks to Natalie and Bob Hassold, owners of Tugboat Alley in Portsmouth, NH, who first came up with the idea for this book.

Thanks to all those individuals who gave me interviews.

We gratefully acknowledge the generous cooperation of the following marine towing companies, their crews and their administrative staffs:

Portland Tugboat	Great Lakes Towing
Moran Towing	Edison Chouest Offshore
McAllister Towing and	Foss Maritime
Transportation	Millennium Maritime
Boston Towing and Transportation	Crowley Marine
Constellation Towing and Marine	Oscar Niemeth Towing
Bay State Towing	Westar Marine Services
Simpson Towing	Shaver Transportation
Wilmington Tug	Smith Maritime
Cape Fear Towing	Fremont Tugboat
E.N. Bisso & Son	Western Towboat
Dolphin Towing	

Special thanks to Captain Ann Kinner of San Diego TowBoatU.S.

Data on the Mississippi River (page 72) courtesy of the National Park Service and "Wikipedia," the free encyclopedia.

Appreciation and thanks to my crew mate and wife, Martha, for accompanying me on much of the two-year voyage on which we traveled to research this book.

Grateful appreciation to Hugh Ware of the Tugboat Enthusiasts' Society for his expertise and for his reading of the material in this book.

Photo Credits

All photos by the author, Warren Salinger, except as noted below:

Page 3, Susan Maycock
Front cover and pages 4–5 (*center*), 9 (*bottom*), 10 (*top left and center*), and back inside flap, all courtesy of Moran Towing;
Page 12 (*top left*), courtesy of Western Towboat
Page 13, courtesy of Edison Chouest Offshore
Page 12 (*bottom right*), 14–15 and 40, Brian Teahen
Pages 19, 20, 25, Robert Hassold
Pages 49 (*bottom*), 51 (*bottom*), 55, 61 (*top*), courtesy of TES (the Tugboat Enthusiasts Society of the Americas) photo library
Page 57 (*top*), courtesy of McAllister Towing and Transportation
Pages 69 and 70, courtesy of E.N. Bisso & Son, Inc. and Bill Summers;
Page 95 (*top*), courtesy of Millennium Maritime;
Pages 122 (*bottom*), 123, 126, courtesy of Western Towboat.
Back cover - author's photo by Robert J. Konieczny, Sr.; Tug picture courtesy of Western Tugboat

Happy Holidays
Christmas 2003
From
Mark & Margie Freeman